The Rise of State Capital

T0326505

Comparative Political Economy
Series Editor: Erik Jones

This series explores contemporary issues in comparative political economy. Pluralistic in approach, the books offer original, theoretically informed analyses of the interaction between politics and economics, and explore the implications for policy at the regional, national and supranational levels.

Published

Central Bank Independence and the Future of the Euro
Panicos Demetriades

Europe and Northern Ireland's Future
Mary C. Murphy

The Magic Money Tree and Other Economic Tales
Lorenzo Forni

A Modern Migration Theory
Peo Hansen

The New Politics of Trade
Alasdair R. Young

The Political Economy of Housing Financialization
Gregory W. Fuller

Populocracy
Catherine Fieschi

Resilient Welfare States in the European Union
Anton Hemerijck and Robin Huguenot- Noël

The Rise of State Capital
Milan Babić

Whatever It Takes
George Papaconstantinou

The Rise of State Capital

Transforming Markets and International Politics

Milan Babić

agenda
publishing

Za Mamu, Tatu, Vanju

© Milan Babić 2023

This work is licensed under a Creative Commons Attribution-NonCommercial-NoDerivatives v4.0 International Licence (CC BY-NC-ND 4.0). Permission for reproduction is granted by the author and publisher free of charge for non-commercial purposes. To view a copy of the licence visit https://creativecommons.org/licenses/by-nc-nd/4.0/.

First published in 2023 by Agenda Publishing

Agenda Publishing Limited
The Core
Bath Lane
Newcastle Helix
Newcastle upon Tyne
NE4 5TF
www.agendapub.com

ISBN 978-1-78821-572-5

British Library Cataloguing-in-Publication Data
A catalogue record for this book is available from the British Library

Typeset by Newgen Publishing UK
Printed and bound in the UK by 4edge

Contents

Acknowledgements

The idea to think about how and why states rise as owners in the global political economy and why we should care about this stems from my doctoral supervisor and friend Eelke Heemskerk. Thanks for being as enthusiastic as one can be from the start to the end of the project that forms the basis for this book. The practical and moral support to materialize this idea into a book stems from my postdoctoral supervisor and friend Adam Dixon. Thanks for your invaluable personal and professional help in bringing this project home. Alison Howson, Erik Jones and Steven Gerrard at Agenda accompanied and supported this project from the beginning, and I thank you for that.

I also want to thank all the people that were involved from close and far away and helped to bring together the research culminating in this book. The CORPNET team at the University of Amsterdam, and the SWFsEUROPE team at Maastricht University accompanied me in those years and taught me a great deal about how the social world works and how we can make sense of it. I thank, in alphabetical order, Lena Ajdacic, Ilias Alami, Jan Fichtner, Javier Garcia-Bernardo, Jouke Huijzer, Imogen Liu, Arjan Reurink, Frank Takes, Diliara Valeeva and Dawid Walentek. Besides being great minds, you are simply extraordinary people and I am fortunate that all of you left your mark on this project. Furthermore, many other bright people helped, read bits and pieces, and gave valuable advice over the years: Roberto Aragao, Brian Burgoon, Malcolm Campbell-Verduyn, Bruce Cronin, Danny DeRock, Annette Freyberg-Inan, Daniel Gomez, Naná de Graaff, Sandy Hager, Joan van Heijster, Eric Helleiner, Otto Holman, Ans Kolk, Lukas Linsi, Chris Luigjes, Elsa Massoc, Daniel Mügge, Andreas Nölke, Henk Overbeek, Wouter Schakel, Philip Schleifer, Gerhard Schnyder, Herman Mark Schwartz, Will Winecoff, Geoffrey Underhill and Matti Ylönen. All errors remain mine, and all smart things said in this book probably came from these people.

Friends and colleagues from the PETGOV group in Amsterdam helped me to refine my ideas by reading, challenging, motivating, inspiring, and sometimes just being around. My postdoctoral colleagues from the GDS group in Maastricht welcomed me warmly in their midst during a pandemic, for which I am grateful. Finally, my new academic home at the Department of Social Sciences and Business at Roskilde University, where this manuscript was finalized, accepted me with open arms and made me excited about joining this vibrant community. I want to thank especially Laura Horn for your help and generosity in all things life and work.

Furthermore, I thank the European Research Council for funding large parts of this research under the European Union's Horizon 2020 research and innovation programme (grant agreement numbers 638946 and 758430). The SWFsEUROPE project and Adam Dixon generously funded the open access option for this book (grant agreement number 758430).

Finally, I thank Sophie and Dana for being here. Ihr seid mein Zuhause.

Foreword

Erik Jones

Modern states are market participants, both at home and abroad. States invest on a massive scale to fund future contingent liabilities. Think not only of sovereign wealth funds, like Norges Bank Investment Management, but also diversified public pension funds, like the California Public Employee's Retirement System. States also invest to secure access to infrastructure or natural resources, often using state-owned enterprises or public–private partnerships to achieve their objectives. And when states participate in markets this way, they become invested in the rules that regulate market transactions, including the rules for dispute resolution. Again, this is true both at home and abroad because states have an interest in protecting the rules that ensure they will profit from and retain control over their investments.

Milan Babić shows how this insight about states as market participants is an essential qualification in the debate about "state capitalism" that has emerged alongside the rise of China as a rival to the United States and Europe within the international economic system. The point, Babić argues, is to think beyond the dichotomy between states and markets to focus on the strategies states use to navigate markets instead. This new focus is particularly important at the global level where enforcement of market rules is shared across powerful states and global economic institutions because those strategies are not neutral. They reflect powerful interests both within and around state institutions. They also reflect ambitions that could bring rival state governments into conflict over access to strategic resources or relative returns on investments.

The war in Ukraine that Russia began in 2014 and intensified in 2022 makes it imperative that we consider the role of states in markets. What we have seen with brutal clarity is how rival states can use shared infrastructures and strategic resources to exercise leverage. We have also seen how they can suddenly change the rules governing both real and financial investments. What is more challenging is to assess the relative strength of the underlying interests at play in these dynamics.

How much the world's leading powers are willing to tolerate or sacrifice to protect a rules-based international economic system is an open question. We can speculate about what are the breaking points that arise as a result of the "weaponization of interdependence", to borrow from Henry Farrell and Abraham Newman, but it remains unclear just how much Russia, China, the United States, European countries, or other powerful states remain "invested" in the global economy and how much they have already decided to retreat to less encompassing, more easily managed market relationships.

Babić's book does not provide a firm answer to these questions, but it does provide the framework necessary for thinking about how they might be answered. In doing so, he shows how state actors, sovereign wealth funds, state-owned enterprises, and para-public institutions operate transnationally in ways that reveal underlying ambitions and competing interests. This argument exposes subtleties that a division of the world into democracies and authoritarian regimes might miss. Babić sets out a research agenda with clear and important policy implications. Anyone looking to anticipate the development of the world economy should read it.

1

Introduction: states and markets are different things – or are they?

State capitalism: what's in a word?

The early twenty-first century was in many ways the perfect unipolar moment. A decade after the end of the Cold War, major events such as the ideological triumph of liberal democracy, the resolution of violent conflicts in the Balkans and elsewhere and the declaration of the UN Millennium Development Goals promised a future in which the United States, as *primus inter pares*, would oversee the supposed end of history. For the global political economy, this unipolar imagination left little room for alternatives to neoliberal globalization.[1] US President Clinton summarized this conviction by stating that "globalization is not something we can hold off or turn off. It is the economic equivalent of a force of nature, like wind or water" (Clinton 2000: 2549). Following this logic, the modern state could only be expected to play a mildly moderating role and be a bystander in the great game of globalization. Western policy-makers and voters seemed to broadly accept that the world is now "flat" (Friedman 2005) – and that alternative ways of organizing their political economies were inconceivable.

---

1. I understand neoliberal globalization here as a historical process that entailed, among others, the reconstitution and liberalization of global financial markets (Helleiner 1994), the deregulation of goods, service and labour markets (Peters 2008), the rollback or restructuring of social welfare systems towards greater flexibility and efficiency (Karimi 2016: ch. 6; Kus 2006) and attempts to increase "national competitiveness", for example through corporate tax competition in many OECD countries (Heimberger 2021). Through this, it privileges certain social purposes over others in favour of corporate capital and asset holders. Chapter 7 discusses this concept in more detail.

It was not long before reality caught up with this imagining. The unipolar project was visibly shattered by 9/11 and the subsequent endless wars waged by America and its allies. But also in the economic realm, alternative modes of organization appeared on the horizon. Countries like Brazil, Russia, India, China and South Africa (collectively known as the BRICS) embraced what has at times been dubbed "state-led market economy", "political capitalism" or most commonly "state capitalism", and seemingly rearticulated the notion of state power in the global economy. Many state capitalist economies developed their own stance towards globalization that was different to what the neoliberal playbook suggested. Instead of submitting state power to quasi-natural economic forces, these countries employed state-led economic tools and practices to deal with the adamant forces of globalization. Soon, academia and media formulated a narrative around their rise: a "war between states and corporations" (Bremmer 2010) was on the horizon; the "return of statism" was "transforming the world" (Kurlantzick 2016); and this would lead to a new state capitalist challenge to the liberal economic order by countries such as the BRICS (see, e.g., Nölke *et al.* 2015). The emergence of a state-led alternative to neoliberal globalization successfully crushed the unipolar moment of the early 2000s. Today, state capitalist economies, spearheaded by China, are expected to tighten the reins of neoliberal globalization in world politics.

In this book, I challenge this narrative of the rise of state capitalism. I argue that it was not primarily statist economies, but rather *state-owned capital*, that rose to prominence in the global political economy. What is commonly described as the state capitalist challenge to neoliberal globalization is in fact a consequence of neoliberal globalization itself. It gave states the ability to become global owners and investors, to enter global markets and to control large assets outside their own borders. As a consequence, the effects of the economic participation of states on international politics are not as straightforward as the narrative of the state capitalist challenge might suggest. States that become global owners are to a large degree invested in the functioning and the rules of a globalized economy. The idea that they represent a countermovement to neoliberal globalization is therefore inaccurate. I contend that the consequences for international politics lie rather in the fact that some states, like China or Norway, have become large cross-border owners in other states, where they compete with other economic actors for relative gains and often cause heated domestic debates about the nature and extent of foreign state ownership. International politics hence becomes more competitive, and global rivalries are exacerbated by the role of states as global owners of capital. This is a different set of issues than the state capitalist challenge suggests. States as different as France, Singapore and Qatar have taken advantage of the opportunity structures offered by neoliberal globalization and compete with each other and other economic actors. They have risen not *against* but *within* neoliberal globalization. It is consequently not the geopolitical battle between rising state capitalists and the liberal West that continues to shape international relations, but rather the geoeconomic competition for relative gains in the global economy.

If the rise of state capitalism is not about a systemic challenge, how does it relate to the undeniably higher relevance of statist economies in world politics? In addition to emerging economies like Brazil or India, this concerns China in particular, which became the prime contender for US hegemony in the last two decades. I do not dispute the profound developments that have taken place and continue to transform world politics. In fact, I expect the global economy to become even more statist in the coming years, not at least because of the socio-economic reverberations of Covid-19 (see Chapter 6). However, I argue that the transformation of states into global owners is not simply an ideological challenge from non-Western states, but a much broader transformation of and within neoliberal globalization. In fact, many large capital-owning states such as Norway or France are part of the very same liberal order that is allegedly challenged by state capitalism. By scrutinizing and nuancing what is commonly referred to as the rise of state capitalism, this book makes sense of these developments by moving beyond a simple dichotomy of world politics.

In this book, I develop a perspective on the rise of state capitalism that takes the political economy of states as owners seriously. I scrutinize conceptually and empirically what it means when states become global owners: how do we measure cross-border state investment adequately? Which strategies do different states employ when they become owners and investors? Where do they invest and how deeply are they invested in different regions and countries? How does cross-border state investment affect international politics beyond the narrative of the state capitalist challenge? These questions are key building blocks of this book. In order to answer them, I draw on both large-scale, firm-level data on state ownership relations and in-depth case studies. I sketch the landscape of the rise of transnational state capital and explore how this rise affects international politics in variegated ways, from geoeconomic competition to climate change. From this analysis, I also formulate an analysis of the role of state capital in a post-Covid world: what can we learn from the rise of states as global owners in the last two decades in dealing with the fallout of the worst natural disaster in a century?

When governments enter markets

Within the social sciences, but especially in public discussions, there is a tendency to look at "states" and "markets" as analytically separate spheres of social life. Although scholarship from different traditions, for example in

International Political Economy (IPE), regularly challenged and questioned this logic, it remains pervasive. For analytical and pedagogical reasons, it is after all useful to think within and through their interplay, from the local to the transnational. However, the phenomenon of state capital is difficult to situate within this distinction. How should we think about states that become investors and shareholders, sometimes even full-scale owners of large multinational corporations? It is meaningless to operate under the assumption that states fulfil classical state roles in this situation: they do not regulate, constrain or enable markets; they reap market benefits, compete with other actors, and create consequences for those markets and international politics at large. They do what market actors do. The rise of transnational state capital – that is, the rise of states as global corporate owners – hence represents a hard empirical and practical problem for making sense of Chinese transnational state-owned enterprises (SOEs), Norwegian sovereign wealth fund investment or Qatari stakes in major global corporations in recent years.

It is perhaps the original analytical distinction between states and markets that produces analyses which frame the rise of state capital(ism) as the emergence of states embracing a particular set of economic policies that are summarized under the label of state capitalism. In order to understand how Brazil, China or Russia organize their political economies today, this is a reasonable approach.[2] What I argue is that the often-employed notion of a "rise" of state capitalism becomes problematic from this perspective. Although in ideological hindsight, "state capitalists" like Russia or Brazil receive more attention in an increasingly multipolar world, they are far from becoming economically more powerful. In essence, there was no real "rise" of state capitalism from this perspective in the last two decades, as I show below: Brazil and Russia did not improve their relative shares of gross domestic product (GDP), exports or other standard indicators in the global economy. The only "state capitalist" that did so was China. Framing the various forms in which states as owners rise in the state–market dichotomy is consequently problematic and leads to a narrow focus on one major example, disregarding the forms of statist rearticulation we see in the global political economy.

These different forms represent the empirical focus of this study. When Swiss agrochemical giant Syngenta was taken over by Chinese state-owned ChemChina in a spectacular $40 billion deal, or when Russian state-owned Rosneft invested a record $13 billion to acquire Indian Essar Oil, each state became a large-scale transnational owner. Through direct, cross-border ownership ties, they inserted

---

2. For the application of this approach in comparative political economy, see, for example, Nölke *et al.* (2019).

themselves into global circuits of investment and corporate control and became part of global markets. This transformation does not per se challenge or transform the global political economy. Rather, states rise within, not against, the structures of neoliberal globalization. As global corporate owners, they leave the iron cage of the nation state in order to reap the benefits of a globalized economy, such as returns on investment or the acquisition of strategic assets. They are able to do so only because of the fact that neoliberal globalization created the respective conditions, for example through the cutback of trade and investment barriers or through the creation of global marketplaces. I call this emerging global arena in which different actors can pursue economic goals the *transnational agency space*. This book scrutinizes how state capital has been able to occupy a part of this emerging space successfully.

Within this space, not all actors are the same. As recent research has demonstrated, powerful states can and do control important networks and other transnational structures within this global space to their benefit (Farrell & Newman 2019). In our case, resource-rich states were able to bundle state capital and reap the benefits of a globalized economy. The fact that states become proactive owners, pushing into global markets and competing with other economic actors, represents a new type of state form. In the 1990s, political economy scholars conceptualized the state form of the *competition state* (Cerny 1997): a set of institutions whose (passive) logic of competitive advantage-seeking is driven by adapting to the merciless forces of neoliberal globalization. I suggest a new state form called the *competing state* to capture the growing presence of states as global owners. Different from the competition state, it uses its vast resources – such as revenues from extractive resources, or large amounts of foreign exchange reserves – to compete for different economic goals, such as returns on investment or technological development. I argue in this book that the competing state, albeit epitomized by only a handful of globally relevant owners, represents a major post-neoliberal state transformation that deviates in important aspects from the competition state of the neoliberal era.

Taken together, the core argument of this book is that what we commonly refer to as the rise of state capitalism against the global liberal order is better captured as a rise of state capital within, and enabled by, neoliberal globalization. The state form emerging from this rise is the competing state, which reaps the benefits of a globalized economy by transforming states into global owners and investors. Although this emergence of the competing state is an argument that questions the narrative of the state capitalist challenge to neoliberal globalization, it does have crucial consequences for international politics. If states become global owners, they enter other jurisdictions as market actors and thereby necessarily create reverberations that go beyond those that "private" actors usually cause. Chapters 4 to 6 deal with these consequences for international politics. In the remainder of this introduction, I present empirical evidence for what I refer to as the rise of transnational state capital and introduce ways of capturing this rise analytically as well as describing the two main concepts of the book, namely the idea of a transnational agency space and of the competing state.

Is there a "rise" of state capital(ism) in the global economy?

In 2012, *The Economist* (2012) published a special report on "The Rise of State Capitalism". In it, the authors summarized a decade of state-led development models in different parts of the world and concluded that state capitalism has changed. Instead of the "old", state-owned conglomerates – often under the direct control of inefficient ministries – state capitalism has produced a considerable number of multinational companies since the end of the 1990s. The most baffling development for *The Economist* seemed to be the rise of transnationally active SOEs and sovereign wealth funds (SWFs) and their "sheer collective might in the emerging world". Large, powerful, state-owned vehicles moved into the realm of global capitalism and successfully competed with their private counterparts for economic gains. State capitalism was no longer a fringe phenomenon in a liberal global economy but competing at the apex of global capitalism.

At the same time, the report reproduced a common trope: it equated the existence and success of those state-owned vehicles with the rise of the political economies from which they stem. It is no surprise then that state capitalism is described as "fatally flawed", as it supposedly only thrives on corruption and nepotism in "problematic states" such as Russia and China. The rise (and possible fall) of state capitalism is, according to this perspective, tied to the rise of a limited number of emerging, statist economies. It made the rise of state capital, in the form of corporations or state investment, synonymous with a group of "statist" development models, such as China, Russia or Brazil. However, although state-owned multinationals do indeed often stem from these countries, they cannot be equated: the Brazilian growth model is not identical with the investment ties Petrobras creates around the world. The difference becomes even more striking when comparing the relatively small economy (by GDP) of Norway with its $1 trillion SWF; and the same holds for other SWFs and their owners, such as the United Arab Emirates or Qatar.

The blending of both phenomena is as pervasive as it is problematic. How do we establish whether state capitalism is really increasing? Following *The Economist*'s report, state capitalism is both rising and not: SOEs are among the largest and most powerful corporations in the global economy, but the political economies from which they stem are less successful compared to their liberal peers. Similarly, SWFs enter and stir up global financial markets, but their owners are often at best what Peter Katzenstein (1985) called "small states in world markets". Moreover, how should we reconcile the alleged state capitalist rise of the BRICS, while ignoring "non-state capitalist" economies with successful state capital transnationalization strategies such as Norway or France? In short, we need to be precise in what we mean when we speak about the rise of state capital(ism).

To get a better grip on the question, we can take a close look at both the rise of state capitalist *economies* and the rise of state-owned *vehicles* in the global economy. For the former, we can consider different macroeconomic indicators for different state capitalist countries. Figure 1.1 shows the state capitalists'[3] share of global GDP, and Figure 1.2 shows their share of global exports over the last two decades.

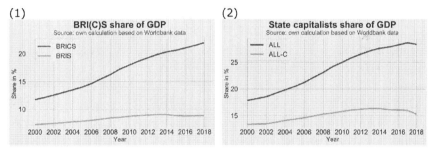

Figure 1.1 (a) BRICs' share of GDP, 2000–18; (b) state capitalists' share of GDP, 2000–18
Source: own calculation based on World Bank data.

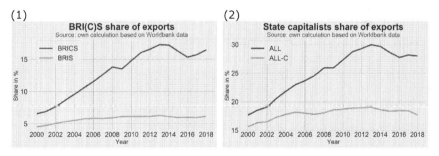

Figure 1.2 (a) BRICs' share of exports, 2000–18; (b) state capitalists' share of exports, 2008–18
Source: own calculation based on World Bank data.

---

3. The sample of state capitalist countries follows the sampling of Kurlantzick (2016: 14), who lists 20 out of the 60 largest economies as state capitalist. The threshold used is that at least a third of the largest companies in a country need to be state controlled. The countries included in this list are the following (sorted by 2016 GDP): China, Brazil, India, Russia, Indonesia, Saudi Arabia, Argentina, Norway, Iran, Thailand, the UAE, Malaysia, Singapore, Egypt, Kazakhstan, Algeria, Qatar, Venezuela, Vietnam, Kuwait.

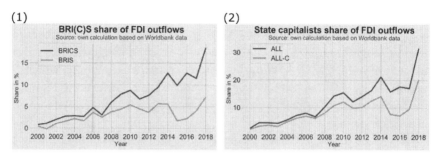

Figure 1.3 (a) BRICs' share of FDI outflows, 2000–18; state capitalists' share of FDI outflows, 2000–18

Source: own calculation based on World Bank data.

It is immediately clear that China is the main driver of both upwards trends. With China, the state capitalists increased their share of global GDP from 17.8 per cent to 28.4 per cent in 2018; without China it went from 13.4 per cent to 15.3 per cent. This is of course much less impressive and only a slight improvement relative to the rest of the world economy. For the BRICS only, this trend is similar (from 7.3 to 8.9 per cent).

Global exports can also be a proxy for the relative relevance within the global economy, as higher export levels usually imply higher revenues for the domestic economy. Here, a similar picture to that of GDP emerges (Figure 1.2): with China, the state capitalist countries increased their share from 17.7 to 28 per cent, whereas this looks very different without China (from 15.6 to 17.7 per cent).

In theory, GDP and exports tell us something about the (annual) performance of a national economy, which can then be compared to the output of another state. However, within globalization, comparing states as closed economic units becomes ever more problematic as cross-border ties increase in their relevance for value creation (Linsi & Mügge 2019). Indicators that describe the international and transnational interaction of economies are shown in Figure 1.3 through the state capitalists' share of global foreign direct investment (FDI) outflows over the last two decades. Whereas in the case of the BRICS, the relative weight of China strongly increases after 2013–14, this is not the case for all state capitalists taken together. In 2018, they represent a fifth of all global FDI outflows (without China).

This rise from close to zero two decades ago is the strongest signal of a rise of state capitalism. FDI is a significant indicator, because it measures the (often) longer-term engagement of economic actors across borders. As opposed to "domestic" indicators such as GDP or exports, FDI captures the volume of *cross-border corporate activity* (aggregated at the national level). The rise

Figure 1.4 State owner share of transnational M&A deals, 2000–18
Source: own calculation based on ORBIS Zephyr data.

of state capitalism takes a specific form: as corporate activity within global capitalism. An increased share of FDI outflows indicates that firms from state capitalist countries strengthen their presence in the global economy. This trend tells us something about both the rise of state capitalism and of state capital. On the one hand, FDI outflows are aggregated at the national level, and here state capitalist economies increased their global share. On the other hand, these outflows are undertaken by firms. Corporations from state capitalist economies integrate into and increase their presence on the global stage.

This focus on the actual actors involved in the rise of state capitalism is useful, albeit still limited. After all, China does still play a significant role here, being responsible for a third of all outflows in 2018. What is more, the firms included here are not limited to state-owned entities, but cover all types, including privately owned ones. In order to understand the rise of state capital, we need to take into account data on *state* investment. A feasible way of doing this is to look at cross-border mergers and acquisitions (M&As), where states are on the acquiring side of the equation. This can tell us whether state activity in the global economy has increased, and whether this increase is mainly driven by China.

Figure 1.4 describes the development of cross-border state-led M&A deals over the last two decades. It involves all deals, in which a state-owned entity (such as an SOE or SWF) acquired another corporation (or part thereof) in another state. As we can see, the share of states as owners rises considerably from a low level in 2000 to almost a fifth of all global deals during the Global Financial Crisis (GFC) of 2008–9. Taking the crisis as a marker, the global share of state-led FDI doubled from on average of 5 per cent before to 10.1 per cent after the crisis. It is important to realize that even if the share decreases in some years, the presence of state capital in the global economy continues to effectively increase, because every increase adds to the actual stock of global state-led FDI[4].

Crucially, the role of China in outwards, state-led FDI reduces to just below one percentage point on average per year. Differing from narratives on the rise of the BRICS, here we can see an increase that is not primarily driven by China. This means that the rise of state capitalism in the global economy is better described as the *rise of state capital*: of states as transnational investors and owners. This perspective allows us to go beyond a state-centrism that looks at statist economies as (closed) units rising to challenge the liberal order. At the same time, a caveat applies here: the ascent of state capital does of course not take place in a vacuum. State-owned vehicles are often bolstered by domestic state capitalist models enabling their growth. The aim of this book is not to explicate this relationship, which has already been done in a lot of excellent research (see, e.g., Nölke 2014). Rather, I seek to excavate what it means when states rise as global owners, which strategies they adapt and what the consequences for international politics are. The scrutiny of what really "rises" when we speak of state capital(ism) is an important exercise that helps us to approach the phenomenon of state capital in a systematic manner.

State capital and other concepts

The following chapters explain how we can measure state capital and describe concepts that can help us to gain a deeper understanding of how states became global owners. Before we get there, some conceptual clarifications are important. "State capital", "states as global owners" and "state capitalism" sound similar but describe different phenomena. The issue this book is concerned with is states becoming global economic owners. This means that states act as corporate shareholders in other countries. What this shareholding looks like – whether an SWF owns a small share of a publicly listed company abroad, or an SOE owns and controls a whole other company somewhere else – and why this matters is discussed in the following. This definition excludes *domestic* state ownership, which is not dealt with here.

I describe the shareholdings a state owns outside its own borders as transnational state capital.[5] In its most basic form, economic capital is *value in motion*,

---

4. The presented numbers are flows, and hence they represent the state share of all FDI going out in a specific year. Since FDI is usually a longer-term investment, each flow adds to the existing stock of cross-border state-led FDI.

5. Since I only focus on cross-border shareholding, I use transnational state capital and state capital interchangeably in this book.

what David Harvey calls money "sent in search for more money" (Harvey 2011: 40). Operationalizing this perpetual process in order to be able to measure it means taking a snapshot at a given point in time. The way I do this is pretty straightforward: if the Russian state owns Gazprom, it controls – at a given moment in time – a certain amount of value outside its own borders. I call this value state capital, because the Russian state controls it via its vehicle Gazprom. There is a specific way of calculating the exact amount of state capital a state holds in a firm, which is detailed in Chapter 3. There, I also describe some of the caveats we need to be aware of when measuring state capital.

If states as owners control state capital outside their own borders, is this state capitalism? Maybe. I prefer to remain agnostic about this question, as a lot of smart people have racked their brains about this issue of defining state capitalism (see, e.g., Alami & Dixon 2020a). The exercise of criticizing the narrative of the rise of state capitalism problematized the concept itself and helped to develop an alternative perspective on what has happened in the global political economy over the last two decades. By saying that states rise as owners, I am able to give a more precise, empirically traceable and politically analysable account than claiming that state capitalism is on the rise. This book consequently deals with the phenomenon of state capital and leaves the broader concept of state capitalism aside for the time being.

The last conceptual clarification concerns the idea that "states" become owners. It is after all state-owned *vehicles* that create the transnational ties I seek to study in this book. Is it fair to say that the Norwegian "state" creates an ownership tie when its (professionally managed) SWF invests outside of Norway? I think it is. To be clear, I do not claim that the Norwegian SWF – or any other state-owned entity – is identical with the Norwegian state. Far from it. But what I am interested in analysing is what happens when states rise as owners in the global political economy. In all datapoints that I gather in this study, and in each example I use, it is a state-owned entity[6] that creates transnational ownership ties. To track state control as closely as possible, I only consider ties created by majority state-owned entities. The following chapters dive deeper into what different strategies states employ on average and how these strategies can be empirically differentiated. For now, it is important to keep in mind that the language employed in this book of "states doing things" refers to the situation of states acting *as economic owners*. If Norway invests, Russia is invested or China transnationalizes its investment, it means that the (majority-controlled) state-owned investment vehicles of these states "do" something.

---

6. This state-owned entity needs to be state controlled by majority, that is, by at least 50.01 per cent state ownership. See Chapter 3 for details on the operationalization.

As their owners, (local or national) governments are involved in these processes, albeit via proxies. In short, by referring to states as actors in this book, I explicitly refer to their role as owners and investors of state capital.

Putting state capital in its place: the structure of the book

Chapters 1–3 lay the groundwork for understanding the historical and material conditions of the rise of state capital and its theoretical implications. Chapter 1 introduces the argument that the rise of state capital is not a movement *against* but *within* neoliberal globalization, and clarifies important definition questions. To understand this specific character of the rise of state capital within neoliberal globalization better, Chapter 2 presents a short history of the rise and fall of state interventionism within global capitalism over the last 100 years. The main argument developed in the chapter is that the so-called third wave of statist rearticulation over the last two decades is in key respects different from earlier rearticulations. This has important implications for how we analyse the rise of transnational state capital empirically. Chapter 3 entails a methodological note on how to operationalize and measure transnational state capital, and it also introduces two key concepts relevant for understanding the rise of state capital. The first is the *transnational agency space* created by neoliberal globalization, which enables states to become large-scale owners and investors. The second is the concept of the *competing state*: by becoming owners, states develop a relationship with globalization that is fundamentally different from the policy repertoire of the competition state of the 1990s and 2000s. The analytical figure of the competing state helps to analyse this transformation and its empirical consequences for international politics.

Furthermore, Chapter 3 delineates seven ideal-typical strategies, ranging from purely "financial" strategies aiming to maximize returns on investment, to "control" strategies aiming to acquire and control corporations and other key assets in the global economy. I delineate these strategies on the basis of the largest firm-level dataset to date.[7] Chapters 4 and 5 then delve into the different strategies that states as global owners employ. Both chapters then each detail some of the largest and most powerful states as owners in order to understand the qualitative side of the strategies these states employ. I embed these strategic profiles in the political economies that they stem from and delineate the global

---

7. I draw on a dataset created from raw Bureau van Dijk's ORBIS database consisting of around a million state ownership relations in total, and around 100,000 transnational ties. More information on the dataset can be found in the References.

political implications of these competing strategies. This is the empirical heart of the book and adds substance to the developed notions of the transnational agency space and the competing state.

Chapter 6 finally looks beyond the state perspective to the international political scene and how the rise of transnational state capital affects international politics in different realms. I survey three main areas of international politics, where state capital plays an increasingly relevant role: the Covid-19 pandemic, geoeconomic competition and climate politics. In the *short term*, the pandemic not only wreaked havoc on many societies around the world, but also distorted global value chains and whole economies on an unprecedented scale. Around the world, states again inserted themselves as lenders, buyers and supporters of last resort, mobilizing vast amounts of money to stabilize their (very different) growth models. What does this supposed "comeback" of the state mean for a post-pandemic world and what role does state capital play within it? I sketch an answer to this question in Chapter 6. In the *medium term*, the rise of states as owners often prompts us to think in terms of geopolitical rivalry, as states mobilize large sums of investment to acquire equity in another country. Inevitably, this leads to questions about the motives and abilities of states to create political and economic leverage over the host state. If, however, we look closely at how and why states transnationalize capital, the geopolitical narrative is often blurred. More often, issues of geoeconomic competition for industrial catch-up or foreign market shares and technologies come to the fore. I explore this geoeconomic dimension in Chapter 6. In the *long term*, state capital also plays a role in efforts to mitigate climate change as the overarching political and social issue of our times. Climate change in international politics is often approached as a regulatory issue: the looming environmental catastrophe needs to be avoided by domestic regulation as well as (often impossible) multilateral cooperation between states. At the same time, many states are large-scale, transnational owners of corporations that sit on the world's largest fossil fuel reserves. In fact, many global owners like China and the Gulf states became large transnational players through their direct or indirect ownership and sale of fossil fuel commodities and the respective technology. It is the more urgent to understand how the transnationalization of state capital is built on a discontinued but still powerful model of energy generation, and what role states as global owners of fossil fuel sources play in the energy transition.

Chapter 7 concludes the book by giving an outlook into what the findings potentially mean for the discussion about the relationship between states and markets. The role of state capital as described in this book is highly ambiguous: it is a means for sovereign states to insert themselves into global circuits of capital. Far from giving up sovereignty, this insertion seems to enable states to adapt to neoliberal globalization without necessarily giving up on state power.

The competing states analysed in this book have all seemed to, at least temporarily, *gain* policy space and competitive advantages through playing the game of globalized capitalism. In the conclusion, I therefore discuss the main argument of this book and its findings in relation to the existing literature on state power within globalized capitalism, and explore the potentials and limits of its articulation in a post-neoliberal world. I argue that while the competing state is only one aspect of how state power functions today, it presents a necessary and important corrective to the idea that neoliberal globalization simply superseded state power. By embedding the argument of the book in a longer and ongoing political economy debate, I hope to introduce both nuance and a new perspective on what state power is and can be in the twenty-first century.

2

A short history of the re-emergence of state capital(ism)

Polanyi in Beijing and beyond

The increasing political importance of the BRICS – and other "state capitalists" – during the first decade of the twenty-first century provoked analyses that drew heavily on what I describe as a "popularized Polanyi-ism". The economist and sociologist Karl Polanyi himself argued that nineteenth-century liberal attempts to "disembed" the economy from the rest of society led to a backlash in the form of "re-embedding" forces in the early twentieth century (Polanyi 2001). In a similar vein, political commentators understood the ascent of neoliberal globalization in the 1980s as an attempt of a global disembedding of markets, which would be met by renewed embedding efforts in the early twenty-first century.[1] State capitalism has been identified as one of those forces that would push back against the neoliberal reach, in the form of the often-cited "return of the state". Typical state capitalists like the BRICS function as the concrete actors of such a popularized Polanyi-ism, in and beyond China.

As plausible as such figures of thought are, they often only scratch the surface of historical developments. Understanding the recent emergence of state capitalism as a phase of the historical ebb and flow of cycles of state intervention and renewed liberalization often means neglecting the historical particularities of each wave. The nineteenth-century period of heavy state intervention, monopolies and state-led industrial conglomerates in catch-up industrialization in Germany and Russia is different from the rise of transnational owners like Kuwait or China in the twenty-first century. In order to account for these

---

1. For an overview see Dale (2012).

historical circumstances, it is important to take a closer look at those different phases of statist rearticulation in the global political economy.

The analytical benefit of such historical comparisons is that they sharpen our view on how to better situate and evaluate the current phase of statist expansion we live in. It is precisely the new, transnational nature of the current state capitalist phase that we can recognize through examining previous waves of statism. As I argued in Chapter 1, states reinvented themselves as owners within the opportunity structures that neoliberal globalization created. In this chapter, I therefore put the different phases of state capitalist expansion in the last century in the context of structural changes of the global political economy. These changes, I argue, are mirrored in the very different tools and techniques that states apply as owners and steerers of capital in the different phases of statist expansion. These expansions reflect transformations of state capabilities and state power, and how the relation between states and markets is being rearranged in phases of structural change (see also Strange 1996).

The following periodization describes the phases in which increased economic state activity occurs *in response and in relation to structural changes in the global political economy*. I pay attention to how states interact with the global political economy through the various tools and state forms emerging in these settings, and how they can be compared over time. I distinguish between three state types that emerged within three different historical statist waves.[2] I dub the first state type emerging towards the end of the nineteenth century the *industrializing state*. Increased state involvement in the global economy resulted from the necessity to industrialize domestic economies and compete with other nations for relative gains in the world economy. The second state type is represented by the *protecting state*. After wartime mobilization and the socio-economic devastation of the first half of the twentieth century, increased state involvement in the economy was employed to protect societies – that is, people, but also domestic economies – from the nineteenth-century experience of the impact of a merciless global economy and its competitive pressures. Finally, the third state type which constitutes the object of this book is represented by the *competing state*. Rising at the beginning of the twenty-first century, the competing state represents the superseding of the competition state of the 1990s. Instead of trying to adapt to neoliberal globalization, the competing state exploits the economic opportunities created by this very globalization. The key strategic tool of the competing state is the employment of transnational state capital in order to reap the benefits of a globalized economy.

---

2. These three waves have been succinctly described by Andreas Nölke elsewhere (Nölke 2014).

What all three state forms have in common is that they represent phases of increased domestic economic state involvement in interaction with the global political economy. This interaction is sometimes confrontational (as with the industrializing state within global rivalries) and sometimes cooperative (like the postwar protecting state thriving under embedded liberalism), but it is in each case shaped by the structural environment and its constraints, within which state involvement increases. I focus on the differences and similarities between each state form regarding the tools they employ and the structures that they operate in. As an example, we can see that both the protecting and the competing state are keen on creating so-called national champions that are important for industrial development. At the same time, the circumstances of both are different: the former pushes industrial champions through industrial policy, whereas the latter achieves this through direct state ownership.

Another important aspect we need to pay attention to is the changing geographies of different state forms: whereas the industrializing state was present in Europe and the North Atlantic sphere, the protecting state became the first truly global state form by stretching into Asia, for example. The competing state is mostly located outside Europe and North America, in so-called emerging economies. These differences show how a popularized Polanyi-ism, as described above, is insufficient to understand the current rise of state capital in the global economy. Each state form I describe developed out of a previous phase, in which state functions, priorities and forms were changed and transformed. But this does not imply that what happens in-between those phases represents a "retraction" of the state. This becomes especially clear during the formation of the neoliberal competition state and its transformation into today's competing state form I delineate below. Table 2.1 gives an overview of the different state forms, the main tools they employ and their geographical scope.

Global rivalries and the birth of the industrializing state in the late nineteenth century

The first wave of increased state activity in the global political economy could only take place in a setting where two conditions were fulfilled: the nation state needed to be the predominant form of societal organization, and industrial capitalism needed to become the globally predominant form of organizing production. Both conditions were in place at the apex of British hegemony in the mid-nineteenth century. The first wave of statism, for which the years from the 1840s onwards are crucial, can be located in the very crisis of this British hegemony.

Table 2.1 Three waves of statist rearticulation in the global political economy

State type	Historical situation	Main features and tools	Interaction with global political economy
Industrializing State (1870s–First World War)	Culmination and crisis of pax Britannica; capitalist rivalries among nation states	Tariffs State ownership and cartelization Protectionism of infant industries Economic nationalism Geography: Europe, USA	Fierce competition of nation states for trade gains, industrial catch-up and later colonial expansion **International space**
Protecting state (1930s–1970s)	Aftermath of Great Depression, Second World War and transition to embedded liberalism	Corporatist arrangements (Scandinavia) New Deal (USA) National champions (western Europe) Industry coordination (Japan) Strong state planning and industry coordination combined with trade liberalization and welfare state (after 1945) Geography: Europe, USA, Japan	Global economy is source of domestic welfare (global cooperation and liberalized trade regime); cross-border finance is potentially destabilizing (Bretton Woods and curbing of global finance) **International space**
Competing state (2000s–?)	Deepened globalization and transnationalization; rise of emerging economies	"State-permeated" economies: close state–business relations and coordination National champions (state owned or coordinated) Sovereign wealth funds, development banks, multinational companies Geography: almost global (especially Middle East, South-East Asia, Europe, Latin America)	Global economy is opportunity space for returns on investment and strategic investment; competing state is restricted to resource-rich and able states **Transnational space**

The first phase of this "imperial century" (Parsons 1999), from 1815 to about 1840, was shaped by the industrial revolution, spearheaded by British predominance in the world economy, and fuelled by steam, coal and steel production. Along with its colonial expansion, the British model rapidly transformed the world economy, and by the 1840s drove forward the expansion of global free trade. The abolition of the Corn Laws in 1846 was the first of many measures implemented by the British government to reduce trade barriers and exploit the lead competitiveness of British industry at the time. By the 1860s, this lead had grown to one-fifth of world manufacturing output and over half of global iron and coal production (Kennedy 1988: 151). The push for a more liberalized trade regime began to take shape in 1860, when the Cobden–Chevalier agreement between the UK and France launched a series of further bilateral trade agreements. The following expansion of these agreements in the 1860s and 1870s created a trade system in which Europe and the USA emerged as central hubs (Hallaert 2015: 359).

This system represented the first wave of globalization and at the same time the zenith of British nineteenth-century economic and political dominance. As the harbinger of the industrial revolution, Britain managed to translate its naval and commercial success in the eighteenth century into a hegemonic position in the global political economy. This project was at the same time an incomplete one: globalization 1.0 was always, as Michael Mann put it, "imperially fractured" (Mann 2012: 41), because it was restricted to the North Atlantic sphere and Britain's colonial ties. These ties became more significant when this first wave of globalization started to dissolve towards the end of the nineteenth century. Britain's main competitors in Europe and the USA gradually switched from simple "Ricardian" development strategies, built on the idea of comparative advantage of raw goods, to so-called Kaldorian strategies of industrialization and protection of infant domestic industries.[3] Whereas features of British hegemony were initially beneficial to those strategies – for example, the possibility of cheaper borrowing through adhering to the Gold Standard – the build-up of industrial capacity elsewhere soon led to a revival of global rivalries.

The clearest sign of this revival was a surge in tariffs from the end of the 1870s onwards, first hitting agricultural and finally industrial products as well. By the 1890s, industrializing countries like the USA or Germany had long abandoned a rapprochement to any form of British liberal hegemony. They switched to employing heavy state coordination and intervention, which resulted, among other things, in a reconcentration of industrial ownership in state hands or the state-sponsored build-up of large banks to support industrial

---

3. For an explanation of these strategies see Schwartz (2018).

capital (Gerschenkron 1962). In addition, those European late industrializers used tariffs and protectionist measures that sought to shield their infant industries from competitive pressures. The first state capitalist wave was born, and it was spearheaded by the industrializing state.

In many ways, this first wave can be understood as a result of the response of other European (and later Asian) economies to British industrialization in their attempts to catch up economically. Competitive industrial build-up and tariffs led to global trade frictions that resulted in a more protectionist (and state-led) global economy at the end of the nineteenth century (Schwartz 2018: 104). The famous German bank and industrial cartels such as in the chemical, iron and steel sectors were created through state coordination (Webb 1980). The French state was more strongly involved in *directly owning* vital parts of the newly industrialized economy (Lekoy-Beaulieu 1913). Importantly, in this first phase of statist expansion in the global economy, states around the world acted and reacted to the opportunity structures created by industrialization and British hegemony: in order to rapidly boost industrial productivity, states employed tariffs, infant industry protection and some form of state-led output maximization, be it through state-coordinated cartelization (Germany), strong domestic market protection (USA) or direct state ownership (France).

This first wave of statism was thus crucially marked by the advent of the industrializing state. State-led industrialization and global competition for both raw materials and production, and later for markets and their value-added products, was the driving force behind this transformation. This state form was in many ways a successful one, as late industrializers were able to catch up and finally leave Britain behind in terms of manufacturing output towards the beginning of the twentieth century. In other ways, the emergence of the industrializing state also laid the conditions for the horrendous clashes that resulted in the First World War. Motivated by global rivalries, often led by a zero-sum game image of international politics, and driven by the imperialist search for profits, European powers entered a spiral of capitalist competition and finally unprecedented destruction. This economic nationalism, protectionism and the part-fusion of heavy industry and political elites facilitated the transition from the industrializing to the military state of the First World War.

From global rivalries to the protecting state in the mid-twentieth century

After this first round of industrialization of the core economies at the time, the industrializing state and its immediate grip on the domestic economy was scaled back at the beginning of the twentieth century. The anti-trust movement in the USA, for example, gained traction during this time, and the Wilson administration started to dismantle tariffs and other trade barriers after its electoral win in 1912. In many European countries, the New Imperialism indicated an alteration of the industrializing state's core functions. State support shifted to overseas expansion, which required a different set of tools than those required for the industrializing state. In the British case, for example, financial capital and the service sector were more central to its colonial expansion than industrial capital (Cain & Hopkins 1987). The First World War transformed the involved states furthermore into war mobilization machines. This role ended abruptly after the war, when a postwar deflationary recession turned into a depression during 1920 and 1921. In this period, many states around the world, like Germany, Russia and other war-torn countries in Europe, were unable to deal with the economic fallout of this prolonged crisis period. War debt, a depleted industrial base, inflationary pressures and pre-war exchange rate problems stalled economic recovery in Europe. It was only through American lending that the 1920s became a somewhat mixed and in some cases even positive period for the world economy.

The decade is generally seen as a liberal period, in which international trade soon bounced back to pre-war levels. However, underlying hegemonic problems riddled the emerging global order. On the one hand, American mass production of consumer goods, bolstered by a converted war industry, fuelled its exports and economic growth: already during the war, the USA surpassed Britain's (purchasing power parity-adjusted) GDP and continued a remarkable economic success story into the twentieth century (Tooze 2014). On the other hand, American economic power was not flanked by higher international responsibility. Running a constant current account surplus during this time, the USA was the largest global surplus nation without the intention (or maybe the ability) to level out global imbalances. In addition, protectionist measures like the Fordney–McCumber tariff of 1922 complicated a sustainable recovery of deficit nations in a war-torn Europe. Massive US loans to Europe helped American exporters, while at the same time aggravating global debt problems and trade imbalances. The USA was a reluctant hegemon in this period, neither wanting to write down Allied debt significantly nor seeking to remain a global lender of last resort after 1929 (like they did after 1945, see Schwartz 2018: 175). In short, the USA did not fill the hegemonic void left by Britain, which further destabilized the global economy in the following Great Depression.

The industrializing state was a faded memory at the end of the tumultuous 1930s. Compared to the massive mobilization of capital, labour and industrial organization during the late nineteenth century, European states and the USA had difficulties containing the fallout of the Great Depression, which only came roughly a decade after a disastrous world war. However, a glimpse of the coming phase of renewed state intervention became visible during and towards the end of the Great Depression. The American New Deal politics demonstrated an unforeseen ability of the US state to massively invest in infrastructure projects, the welfare state and progressive taxation and spearheaded a huge expansion of the American economy after a devastating depression. Another example was the Swedish growth model, based on a strong and broad welfare state, which was forged in the crisis-ridden 1930s (Lundberg & Åmark 2001). In both cases, a renewed economic expansion of state activity superseded an era of economic and political turmoil and crisis that paralysed Europe and the USA for more than two decades.

The Second World War again created a situation in which state capacity was employed for military mobilization. The final breakthrough of the protecting state came with the end of the war and the consolidation of American hegemony in the following years. This second wave of state-led economic expansion differed considerably from the first, given that state instruments were no longer used to protect infant industries and resolve global rivalries, but to shield societies from the devastating effects of a liberalized global economy pre-1945. The economic and social catastrophes from the interwar period demonstrated two crucial insights to policy-makers. First, that zero-sum international competition for military and economic gains had adverse domestic effects and that international cooperation should be the cornerstone of a future world order. This crucially involved the enabling of international trade flows and their welfare effects. Second, unregulated cross-border financial flows had the tendency to destabilize domestic economies and were to be limited as far as possible. This should also prevent competitive exchange rate adjustments as well as the worsening of international debt imbalances.

The postwar practice of embedded liberalism, as institutionalized in the Bretton Woods agreement, combined both concerns in a liberalized trade regime (and its welfare effects) with the restriction of cross-border capital flows and a strong state hand in the domestic economy (Ruggie 1982). This intervention took a variety of forms, among which were the previously mentioned US New Deal politics and Swedish welfare state creation, resulting in a renewed expansion of economic state activity, this time with an almost global coverage. In Europe, several types of state involvement played a decisive role in its postwar catch-up with the USA until the 1970s. State-led corporatist coordination in states such as Germany, the Netherlands and Scandinavia ensured that moderate levels of wage suppression were accompanied by large amounts of targeted investment needed to realize this catch-up (Eichengreen & Vazquez 2000). At the same time, extended welfare states ensured that the growing pie of economic success was distributed more equally than in the pre-war period, and that societies were buffered from the adverse effects of the potential volatility of labour markets.

On top of this welfare expansion, many European states began to create national industrial policy strategies that also crucially involved the building up of national champions. These were corporate giants that dominated industries from aerospace (France, UK), aluminium and steel (UK, Germany, France) and automobiles (Italy, Germany, France), to early information technology (UK, France, Germany, the Netherlands) (Vernon 1974). Besides protecting and subsidizing these industries at home, national champions were also internationally relevant. Postwar industrial policy acted as a means of boosting the overall competitiveness of national champions, always with one eye on catching up with the USA. This took different forms in different European states, from a strong presence of direct state ownership in Italy and Austria, to a centralized wage control system in the Netherlands (Shonfield 1969).

Outside of Europe, the Japanese state employed a fine-tuned development model that integrated some of the above-mentioned elements and added others. Critical for its postwar success was the creation of the state-owned Japan Development Bank (JDB) that provided long-term funding for the Japanese industry in a low-savings environment (Yasuda 1993). The JDB was at the core of the efforts of the Japanese state to channel scarce capital to heavy industry that was key for economic development. In this way, postwar Japan was able to solve some of the major coordination issues known as "Gerschenkronian" collective action problems (Schwartz 2018: 88). Instead of relying on market-based financing of industrial activity, the Japanese state was involved in creating the conditions for a more planned distribution of investment after the war. Later, the particular *keiretsu* networks of corporate organization and mutual control took over a large part of these coordination tasks. Together with innovations at the assembly line and skills training (Schwartz 2018: 306), Japan managed to become the prime challenger to the US economy in the 1980s. Statist intervention and ownership after 1945 provided a stable foundation for this rapid development.

The second wave of statist intervention effecting the global economy was in sum marked by a variety of instruments and practices, as states all over the world took a stronger grip on their economies. These ranged from the enormous investment and employment politics of the US New Deal era, the expansion of European welfare states and corporatist arrangements and the initial development of national industrial policies and national champions, to a state-led fine-tuning of comprehensive development strategies. Many of those projects had a decisively inward-looking character, since they were devised to rebuild their war-torn domestic economies. At the same time, the existing soft protectionism and global coordination of issues like exchange rate stability and free trade demonstrate that this rebound of the state also had an international character. Different from the first wave of statist intervention, the second was not born out of the necessity to industrialize and meet emerging global rivalries. On the contrary, the *protecting state* of the second wave employed techniques of state intervention and state ownership in order to shield postwar societies from the brutal impact of a depression and the following socio-economic distortions. As argued above, this protecting function was not limited to an extended welfare state or heavily suppressing cross-border financial flows, but also involved proactive industrial policy and the build-up of internationally competitive national champions. The protective elements of this rebound of the state concerned both society and the economy. The policies of protecting recovering and developing industries from financial instability, as well as from fierce international competition, also extended to the protection of citizens from economic hardship (e.g. via the full-employment policies devised by many states; see Arndt 1994). In sum, the protecting state developed new tools and new vigour in transforming the postwar global economy into a high-growth, high-socially protective environment within the international institutional framework of embedded liberalism.

After neoliberalism: from the competition to the competing state in the twenty-first century

The postwar development model embraced by large parts of Europe, North America and Asia evolved into an existential crisis during the 1970s. The structural problems of the North Atlantic sphere as the heartland of global capitalism were hard to overlook. Inflation levels in the USA, the epicentre of the global economy, rose from very low (and in some years even negative) rates in the 1950s and 1960s to a surge in the 1970s, up to more than 11 per cent towards the end of the decade, heralding the age of sustained inflation (Figure 2.1). The oil price hikes of the 1970s constituted a considerable supply-side shock that translated international conflict into economic reality for consumers. The start of a secular productivity growth decline in the Western world also has its beginning in this decade (Figure 2.2). This decline clashed with the wage demands of strong unions and an organized labour force in the West, leading to a phase of the most intense and continuous industrial conflicts in Europe.

This crisis of the postwar North Atlantic development model took place within the course of major global transformations. The *de facto* dissolution of the postwar Bretton Woods institutional framework by President Nixon in 1971 marked a deep cut into the *modus operandi* of American hegemony.

Figure 2.1 US inflation rate in consumer prices, 1960–90 (annual %)
Source: own calculation based on World Bank and International Monetary Fund (IMF) data.

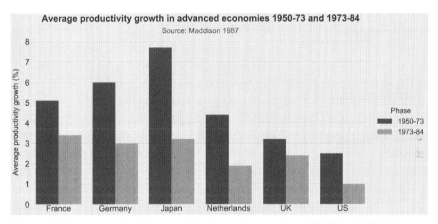

Figure 2.2 Average productivity growth in advanced economies, 1950–73 and 1973–84
Source: Maddison (1987).

The American current account deficit, emerging from capital outflows to Europe and into Eurodollar markets, became unsustainable by the end of the 1960s. The seemingly boundless ability of the American state to supply the world with its currency was overturned when it became obvious that the massive amount of US dollars overseas exceeded the gold reserves held at home (Schwartz 2018: 211). The cutting loose of global exchange rates and the abolition of dollar-to-gold convertibility not only marked the end of Bretton Woods, but also had a lasting transformative effect on the role of the state in economic development.

The protecting state entered a double crisis: on the one hand, the demands directed towards the state in the developed world became strongly politicized. Conservative forces portrayed the modern state as being overwhelmed and its authority undermined by the sheer weight of demands made by various interest groups through democratic procedures (Crozier *et al.* 1975). Critics asserted that this demand inflation made the modern protective state ungovernable. One of the most important indicators for this ungovernability thesis was government expenditure (*ibid.*: 164): a core feature of the interventionist toolbox of the protective state. This critique became a long-lasting conservative argument for reducing the demands from various social groups vis-à-vis the state, and advocating for "small government".

On the other hand, state activity itself became problematic. State intervention and economic planning became the bogeyman during the neoliberal reckoning that took place at the end of the 1970s. Conservative leaders like Margaret Thatcher (UK) and Ronald Reagan (USA) embraced policies that forced back redistributive and social policies for the sake of a more deregulated economy, especially in financial and labour markets. A common misconception is to understand the neoliberal agenda as an assault on the state in order to replace it with a sort of market governance. As current research shows, we should understand neoliberalism better as a political theory which at its core holds that state power should be employed to guarantee the existence and freedom of markets and market participants (Biebricher 2018: 33ff.). For neoliberals, state power is thus an essential tool: it can be employed to crush union power as in Thatcher's Britain, to deregulate labour markets as in many European countries in the 1990s or to counterbalance tax breaks and military spending by tripling national debt as in the USA during the Reagan years. Quinn Slobodian (2018) summarized the core idea of neoliberal politics as isolating the global economy from popular/political influences and "encasing" it at the transnational level through various institutions (such as the World Trade Organization (WTO) or trade and investment treaties). In this way, state power is not primarily abandoning society to markets forces in a Polanyian way, but is actively employed to transform society and institutions in order to protect markets. This form of state reorganization has been described as the "neoliberalization of state space" (Peck 2001), where the protecting state is transformed by the dismantling of some guiding principles of the postwar era related to social security or industrial policy-making.

The specific state form that evolved out of this neoliberalization of state space has been coined the "competition state" (Cerny 1997). As explained closer in Chapter 3, the competition state shifts state priorities from providing social and economic security to its citizens towards making this very society fit to meet the adamant forces of neoliberal globalization. To this end, social and regulatory standards need to be lowered or at least made more flexible to allow the domestic economy to attract foreign investment and "make society fit for competition" (Genschel & Seelkopf 2015: 237). Some of the proponents of the competition state thesis go as far as stating that the advent of globalization changed the very raison d'être of the modern nation state: instead of deriving its rationality from domestic ideas of sovereignty, the competition state derives its rationality primarily from preparing societies to cope with globalization (Cerny 2010). This strong reading suggests that the forces of globalization are so powerful that they dismantle and transform century-old rationalities and state legitimacy. The concept of the competing state, which I discuss in the following chapter, challenges these notions and argues for thinking beyond this state form in the light of the (later) rise of transnational state capital.

The 1990s were a critical period for the transformation towards the competition state. The end of the Cold War and the full unleashing of corporate and cultural globalization seemed to endorse the neoliberal idea of transforming the protective into the competition state. US growth came back on track after the dire 1970s and 1980s and hit an average of 4.1 per cent in the second half of the decade (DeLong 2000). New productivity boosts and decreasing unemployment numbers created an image of the "Roaring Nineties", which added to the notion that the unleashing of neoliberal globalization was a sweeping success. In regions like Southeast and East Asia (especially China), export-driven growth models successfully entered the global economy and profited from it. As an example, the Chinese share of global manufacturing output increased from 2.7 to 7 per cent (Crafts 2006), whereas South Korean productivity grew spectacularly by 49 per cent on average during the decade[4].

In Europe, steady but modest economic growth was outshone by the creation of the European Union (EU) in 1992 and the prospects of the Economic and Monetary Union at the end of the decade. Core elements of the post-Maastricht European integration process are prime examples of the supranational or transnational "encasement" of economic policy-making, such as the Stability and Growth Pact from 1997 or the Maastricht convergence criteria. These elements of what Stephen Gill called a "new constitutionalism" (Gill 1998), which locked in neoliberal policies, were again only made possible through massive interstate bargaining efforts. Even if the competition state is often portrayed as a rather passive agent, employed to reduce and lower standards in order to attract capital and induce growth, many of the neoliberal-era reforms required heavy state involvement and supranational coordination. Beyond the EU integration process, this was especially the case for large free

---

4. Own calculation based on data from Feenstra *et al.* (2015).

trade agreements like the North American Free Trade Agreement between Canada, Mexico and the USA in 1994.

Although the 1990s were generally perceived as the final triumph of globalization and liberal democracy, history did not end after 1989. In opposition to the many successful development stories such as China, other trajectories pointed to the fragile success of neoliberal globalization. Financial crises in Asia (1997), Brazil and Russia (1998) and Turkey (2000) made this fragility painfully clear. Furthermore, regions like sub-Saharan Africa, parts of Latin America or eastern Europe, and South Asia either stagnated or deteriorated in material terms during the 1990s (Zagha 2005: 3). The Russian experience of a lost and chaotic decade was as real as the material stagnation of parts of the lower and middle classes of the developed world during this period. The mixed results of the first truly globalizing decade illustrate that, outside of the core of the global political economy, the ways to catch up, develop and grow economically were not straightforward. Adopting competition state strategies turned out to accelerate existing structural problems and often consolidated existing power asymmetries in the international system. Countries in Latin America and Asia experienced the structural adjustments that came with IMF loans in the 1980s and 1990s, often as one-sided policy scripts from the playbook of the Washington Consensus. The Washington Consensus reflected many of the policy principles of the competition state, such as fiscal discipline, trade liberalization, labour, product and financial market deregulation and widespread privatization (Williamson 1990). The reality of IMF and World Bank adjustment programmes was much messier and more incoherent than the initial ideas on paper, and the responses of the states at the receiving end were more variegated than commonly perceived (Grugel *et al.* 2008: 506). The outcomes were also mostly ambiguous: the initial goal of budget deficit reductions were often achieved, as well as inflation reductions and debt servicing, whereas the social and health costs for the populations were often adverse (Forster *et al.* 2019).

By the beginning of the 2000s, the critique of the role of the IMF and other international financial institutions (IFIs) in promoting competition state politics in its programme countries reached its peak in the developing world. Increased South–South cooperation led to experimenting with new instruments that moved away from the competition state toolbox, such as the employment of SOEs as development tools. Other instruments were the building up of international reserves, quick repayment of IMF loans to escape conditionality, a stronger regional (and international, see BRICS) cooperation and later pushing for reforms of the IMF itself. In Latin America, a strong left nationalism rose as a counter-programme to Washington Consensus politics, which also involved the renationalization of oil and other industries, as in the

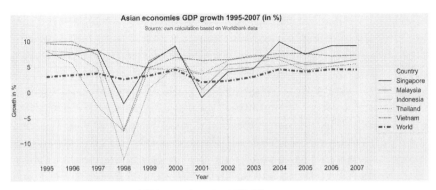

Figure 2.3 Asian economies' GDP growth, 1995–2007 (%)
Source: own calculation based on World Bank data.

Venezuelan case, or the extension of social programmes and welfare, as in Brazil. The results of nationalizing unlikely industries, like finance in Bolivia, gained those states additional policy space in their development trajectories (Naqvi 2021).

The Asian experience was slightly different, as the short engagement with IFI programmes was ended after a sobering experience during the financial crisis of 1997. An influential tradition of sovereignty and non-interference in the region (Grugel *et al.* 2008: 516) shifted the post-crisis rebuilding away from liberalization to more statist forms of development. Cases like Malaysia and Thailand, Vietnam, Indonesia and Singapore employed decisively statist and state-led growth models and were able to sustain growth rates above the global average from the mid-1990s (Figure 2.3).

Asian and Latin American economies were not the only ones turning away from competition state policies and embracing a more statist development model. From the beginning of the twenty-first century up to the GFC and Great Recession starting in 2007, state intervention became the primary tool for emerging markets' development strategies. The most paradigmatic cases of the existence of such a model were the BRICS states. The emergence of those large emerging economies has been described as being "among the most important contemporary structural changes in the global political economy" (Nölke *et al.* 2015: 538). As I argued in Chapter 1, this emergence is not necessarily to be located in the questionable relative rise of those states in the global political economy. Rather, the significance of the BRICS lies in the promotion of a distinct "state-permeated" variant of capitalism as a model for emerging economies. This variant is characterized by close ties between state apparatuses and the business community with regard to corporate governance, corporate finance, labour relations, innovation policies and transnational economic integration (Nölke *et al.* 2019). Different from liberal or coordinated market economies, state-permeated capitalism relies much more on domestic corporate networks, domestically sourced funds for financing business and large domestic markets that allow for industrial development. This reliance on the domestic economy does not, however, imply a protectionist stance, but rather the opposite. Multinational companies from emerging economies are among the largest in their global industries, such as Chinese energy firm CNPC, Brazilian Petrobras, Russian Gazprom or Swiss/Chinese Syngenta. The competitiveness and success of these state-owned multinationals is made possible by the close domestic ties between state and business, bolstering and promoting these transnational state-owned champions. State-permeated capitalism is thus much more than a domestic development model, but it is also crucially intertwined with the global economy.

This interdependence is all the more striking when it comes to SWFs and their sponsor states, which became relevant in the early twenty-first century. The SWF assets under management (AuM) rose from under $1 trillion at the beginning of the decade to over $7 trillion at the end of 2018 (SWFI 2019). This is more than double the $3 trillion AuM held by hedge funds at the end of 2019 (Barclay Hedge 2019). Whereas not all of these assets are held overseas, a core function of SWF investment is to generate returns on (equity) investment. Since the lion's share of SWFs is owned and controlled by emerging market economies, this type of revenue-generating investment is often found cross-border. By these means, SWFs became one of the main tools facilitating the rise of the new statism in the twenty-first century.

This growth of emerging market multinationals and SWFs before the Great Recession was already considerable, but it took the GFC to introduce them fully to the global scene. The GFC is crucial for the ascent of the competing state in two ways. First, it laid bare the enormous size and power of SWFs and other state-owned vehicles when they acted as welcome sources of liquidity for distressed US financial institutions. As an example, sovereign investment from Singapore, South Korea and oil-rich Gulf states served as life-saving capital injections for Citigroup and Merrill Lynch in 2008 (Quinn 2008). These, and other states like China, sat on large foreign exchange reserves that could now function as global capital reserves that were relatively unscathed from the fallout of the American subprime crisis. Second, in addition to the advance of statist vehicles from emerging markets, "Western" institutions also gained more prominence in global financial markets. The most relevant is the Norwegian oil SWF which managed to quadruple its market valuation since the GFC. Whereas this explosion can be partly explained by the immense inflation of asset prices since the GFC (which benefits large asset holders), the rise of transnational state capital from developed countries can also be seen in examples like the inroads the Dutch, German and French states have made into the

British transportation market. Furthermore, state involvement in cross-border M&As reached a peak of over a fifth of all global transactions during the GFC. States rose as global investors and owners, well beyond the realm of emerging economies. The GFC altered the "state–capital nexus" (van Apeldoorn *et al.* 2012) in developed economies around the world.

This tendency has gained more momentum since 2016, when the Brexit referendum and the election of Donald Trump exacerbated global tensions. Whereas both events are not directly connected to intensifying global rivalries, they are important side effects of a longer-term development. Constantly decreasing FDI inflows since 2015 (UNCTAD 2019: 2) reflect a deeper crisis of neoliberal globalization and global economic integration. After years of trade wars, electoral pushbacks against different aspects of globalization and increasing protectionism on a global scale, states are rediscovering tools like industrial policy planning or state ownership. In the EU, voices for a more protectionist stance towards foreign competition are gaining new ground. This stance ranges from proposing rather direct measures like curbing foreign state-led investment, to long-term strategic ideas such as creating state-owned funds that protect domestic firms from foreign takeovers. It is probable that a global Covid-19-induced economic crisis will only accelerate these developments towards renewed global rivalries, in which statist intervention will play a key part.

Overall, the period of increased state intervention since 2000 is thus much more than just a rebound of the developmental state. It is a third wave of statism, which is global in nature. The tools employed in this wave are some that are recognizable from the twentieth century, like industrial policy, state intervention in domestic business and labour relations, and increased state ownership. What truly distinguishes the current wave from the previous ones is its clearly *transnational* character. Whereas the industrializing and the protecting states also interacted with the global economy, they did so via *international* forms. Agents of the industrializing state understood the international environment as a space of potential and real competition for primary goods and industrial development. Industrialization was only possible through massive imports of raw materials and, quite often, labour for the production process, whereas at the same time the protection of infant industries led to a protectionist, often zero-sum stance towards international cooperation. The agents of the protecting state of the twentieth century understood the international environment as an instrument for boosting domestic welfare through a relatively liberal trade regime, but they were also wary of the volatile nature of cross-border financial flows. These flows depicted a source of potential instability and societies and economies were therefore to be protected from the adverse effects of a highly financialized world economy. The competing state of the twenty-first century is located in a very different structural environment: it rose in the 2000s in an increasingly globalized economy which is a much more integrated and qualitatively different space from the old, internationalized world economy (Robinson 2004). This means that the agents steering competing states employ new tools. They create sovereign investment funds to benefit from financial returns on investments on global capital markets, successfully internationalize their SOEs to become competitive global brands and actively support politics that promote outward, as well as inward, FDI flows. States hence competitively employ different tools to reap the benefits of a globalized economy. In some ways, this competitive stance resembles the era of global rivalries in which the industrializing state found itself competing with other states for industrial catch-up vis-à-vis Britain. The difference to today's structural environment lies in its transnationality and the emerging transnational agency space that enables states to become global owners.

On the uses and abuses of historical analogies

Allow me one concluding remark to this whistle-stop tour through history. I want to emphasize that I understand metamorphoses of the state, as described here, not as categorical and neatly separable historical phases. On the contrary, many state forms overlap and influence each other. In fact, I believe that the competition and competing state in particular are inseparable, as they present two alternative reactions of states to neoliberal globalization. What I aimed for with these distinctions and comparisons is to illustrate how structure and agency evolve in their interplay in the global political economy, and to sharpen our perception of how these interactions produce different behaviours and outcomes over time. It speaks for itself that the concepts with which we capture these differences are necessarily blurred, overlapping or simply just ideal-typical to some degree.

This short history puts today's state form of the competing state into perspective. As I have argued, the competing state is neither yet another "comeback of the state" nor an ahistorical state form. Rather, this historical account delineated how we can think about the transformations, breaks and continuities of state power in a comparative manner, without stretching historical analogies too far. What clearly distinguishes the competing state from previous rearticulations of state power in the global political economy is its undeniably transnational character. This makes the competing state an especially contested state form, which is often involved in geopolitical disputes, as state capital moved across borders tends to elicit such reactions. The following chapters attempt to excavate the sources and consequences of these political contestations and to put them into a global perspective.

3

Transnational state capital in the global political economy

From history to the present

The previous chapter developed one key argument: today's rearticulation of state power and its interaction with the global political economy are qualitatively different from previous "waves" of statism. The rise of state capital in its transnational form challenges our existing tools and concepts, with which research in international studies usually grasps real-world phenomena. The vehicles that states as owners use today – SWFs, transnational SOEs, cross-border development banks and others – are relatively new tools at their disposal. This means that new ways of measuring the reach of states into the global economy are needed. At the same time, the emergence of states as global owners poses conceptual confusion: how can we adequately grasp state capital in a way that does justice to the "polymorphism" (Alami & Dixon 2020a: 71) of the phenomenon itself? In this chapter, I clarify this and other questions that help us to better understand transnational state capital as a real-world phenomenon. To this end, I first delineate and discuss two key concepts – the transnational agency space and the competing state – that give us a better idea of how state capital operates, and which new state form follows from this. Afterwards, I describe a straightforward way of measuring transnational state capital on the basis of firm-level ownership data. This measurement tutorial is the basis for the subsequent empirical description of the main strategies states employ as global owners to enter the global political economy. I develop a typology of different strategies – ranging from purely "financial" to more "controlling" interests – which help us in grasping the variety of ways in which states can transnationalize their capital. I also discuss some general descriptive trends of state capital transnationalization on a global scale, which forms the background from which I delve into the different case studies in the following chapters.

Where does state capital rise? A transnational agency space

The argument regarding the particularity of transnational state capital made in Chapter 2 built on the idea that neoliberal globalization enables new forms of statist rearticulation in the global political economy. More precisely, I argue that the rise of state capital could only happen in a global economy that has been profoundly shaped by decades of neoliberal globalization. Transnational state capital could not play a role in a world economy pre-globalization, which consisted of the sum of all nationally bounded economies that interacted with each other (e.g. through a liberalized trade regime). In such a world, the economic role of the state was mostly limited to the iron cage of the domestic economy. Neoliberal globalization breaks with this condition and enables capital – and the actors steering it – to engage in transnational forms of economic interaction. Compared to previous phases of (mostly trade) globalization, neoliberal globalization created the first truly transnational forms of economic activity that are of a permanent nature. The unprecedented growth of FDI flows and stocks and the creation of globally integrated value chains, as well as the emergence of a truly transnational group of finance and legal professionals, managers and corporate owners, are the most obvious factors that distinguish transnational capitalism *qualitatively* from previous waves of globalization (see also Robinson 2004).

Concretely, (state) capital can use a series of transnational opportunity structures that facilitate its rise. Some of the key opportunity structures are:

- The absence of trade and investment barriers – or the existence of trade and investment treaties – between states or regions. This gives corporations not only the opportunity to exchange goods, but to organize long value chains through intra-firm trade, which can be used, among other things, to minimize operational costs.
- The opportunity to access and invest in globalized financial and equity markets in order to gain higher returns on investment than in domestic markets.
- The opportunity to engage in acquiring specialized knowledge, know-how and technological assets through cross-border investment or M&As.
- The existence of a framework of international investor protection that guarantees legal security and allows corporations to file claims against host states.
- The opportunity for firms to borrow and thus finance and leverage their operations through global financial markets and other institutions that were inaccessible before.

- The possibility for companies and highly skilled individuals to migrate between different jurisdictions and also to exploit legal loopholes between those jurisdictions for corporate profit, as is the case for the group of highly specialized tax professionals and their firms.

These and further opportunity structures form the global infrastructure of neoliberal globalization created in the last decades. I dub the entirety of this infrastructure a *transnational agency space*. In it, different economic actors can move in a way that is relatively free from the shackles of the old, domestically oriented world economy. This space is not to be understood in a physical sense, but as the sum of opportunity structures created through neoliberal globalization. The transnational agency space is also not an even space in the sense of a level playing field. As economic geography teaches us, socio-economic spaces are structured by inequality and power relations that have consequences for which actors are more likely to see their interests being realized. The same applies for the transnational agency space that neoliberal globalization created: well-funded corporate actors that are able and willing to exploit transnational connections and opportunities to their benefit are in a different position than many other, much less mobile actors (such as a large part of the global labour force).

This idea of a transnational agency space is inspired by work that aims to capture the *qualitative* spatial shift that occurred with neoliberal globalization.[1] Jan Aart Scholte describes globalization as primarily a spatial transformation: it creates a "globality" that "identifies the planet ... as a site of social relations in its own right" (Scholte 2005: 3). This is a simple but powerful idea. The globalization of particular social relations means that they cannot be satisfactorily explained by territorial consideration any more. They take on a quality of their own, which makes it necessary to find new explanatory patterns. Globality does not, however, imply that territorial relations, and especially their interplay with supraterritoriality, disappear. On the contrary, they can come even more to the fore in times when crises of globalization and nationalist backlashes question global forms of interdependence between states, social groups and other actors.

For the transnational agency space this means that it is not a fixed, physical entity that cannot be altered, such as state borders that are hard to change. The different opportunity structures should rather be understood as channels through which states as owners can invest outside their own borders.

---

1. See for example the landmark studies by Peck & Tickell (2002), Robinson (2004) and van Apeldoorn (2002).

Many of those channels are legal constructs – for example, trade and investment agreements – that could theoretically be shut down politically. The transnational agency space is hence an often fragile and historically evolved global structure that is not strictly defined. It is supraterritorial because it not only demarcates international relations, but involves a variety of truly global aspects that are not reducible to international relations. Transnational state capital is a case in point. If, hypothetically, a Chinese local government decides to acquire a German manufacturing firm, these relations are not primarily a matter between Germany and China: the local government might have a certain degree of independence from the central government, and it will aim for the German firm for a variety of reasons (e.g. to acquire a certain technology or asset). Similarly, the firm might not have anything to do with the federal government and agree to the acquisition out of an economic rationale (e.g. to gain access to Chinese markets). At the same time, these transnational and supranational capital movements might have domestic political backlashes. German politicians might fear the sellout of world-leading technological know-how and try to block the acquisition, while the Chinese central government might feel the need to adapt parts of its going-out strategy in the light of these developments. I discuss such geoeconomic reverberations resulting from transnational state investment closer in Chapter 6. It is important to realize here that different scales of the local, national, international and transnational can be intertwined when it comes to movements within the transnational agency space. However, this space forms the background for even the possibility of such developments: the Chinese local government needs to have the ability and possibility to even attempt to acquire the German company.

The transnational agency space forms the structural background for the rise of transnational state capital. It is the opportunity structures this space offers that enable states to become global owners and move capital through the global economy. Such a relation of state power and neoliberal globalization is quite remarkable. As described in Chapter 2, the dominant political discourse of the 1990s and 2000s circled around the idea of the competition state, which was a rather passive state form. While the opportunity structures of neoliberal globalization have crucially been built by state power, states remained for a long time in the role of enabler and regulator of this space during the heyday of neoliberal globalization. The competition state did not, however, intervene significantly within this space, as it used to do within the domestic boundaries of the old world economy. The emergence of an ever more integrated global economic architecture turned states in many respects into the architects of, instead of actors in, the great game of globalization. Their policy repertoire focused on strategies to adapt to neoliberal globalization, mainly by creating and maintaining supply-side conditions boosting national competitiveness

(Genschel & Seelkopf 2015). How did we get from this state form to what I dub the competing state in the twenty-first century?

From the competition to the competing state

So far in this chapter, I have discussed the structural background to the emergence of transnational state capital. This raises the question of agency: if neoliberal globalization enables state capital to grow, what does this tell us about states as global owners? If we do not want "state capital" to remain an abstract force, it is necessary to conceptualize how this development transforms our understanding of the role of the state in globalization. I call this emerging state form the *competing state*.

In Chapter 1, I clarified that I am concerned with states as owners in this book, not transformations of "the" state as a whole, unitary actor. The emergence of the competing state I describe in the following deals with a transformation in this respect. It tells us something about the changing relationship between resource-rich and financially powerful states and a globalized economy. I do not claim that this transformation supersedes the other relations in which states and globalization interact. Neither do I claim that every state becomes likewise a competing state. Rather, on the contrary, the competing state requires a set of instruments and assets that are not available to most nation states globally. But the concept of the competing state is an important tool to grasp what it means when some states manage to turn the tables and themselves become active global market participants, instead of solely being pressured into the competition state straightjacket. The competing state is hence, in many respects, the dialectical answer to the competition state.

Looking back 20 or 30 years, we cannot discern anything resembling such a proactive state form as the competing state. Across the board, states have been constrained in their policy options with the advent of neoliberal globalization from the late 1970s onwards. The policy space for welfare programmes, industrial policy or other forms of statist economic policy was perceived to shrink, and in the early 1990s (at the latest), states shifted policy capacities to invest in international competitiveness.[2] This meant focusing on the nation state as the analytical unit, which was understood as competing with other states for relative gains in the global economy. The nature of this competition

---

2. For a nuanced narrative on the shift from "first-generation" to "second-generation" neo-liberals, and thus a transformation of the neoliberal project itself, see the excellent account by Linsi (2020).

is, however, indirect: states need to create, maintain and constantly improve a business environment that is capable of ever-increasing productivity (which was in turn supposed to ever increase living standards).[3] The idea of equating competitiveness with national productivity was harshly criticized at the time (e.g. Krugman 1994) but shaped policy-making throughout the 1990s and gave birth to the analytical figure of the *competition state* (Cerny 1997; Davies 2017).

The advocates of the competition state begin with a simple assumption: globalization created a "flat world" (Friedman 2005), similar to the unipolar imagination described above, in which the importance of national (and hence economic) borders for capital accumulation decreases. Instead of states dictating economic policies and keeping corporations in check within their own borders, a globalized economy allows capital to move between jurisdictions and select its preferred destination. The "death of distance" (Cairncross 2001) through technological progress, flanked by the cutback of political barriers to capital mobility (like tariffs or inward FDI protectionism), makes multinational firms – instead of states – central and powerful agents in the global economy. The global political economy consists, in the vision of competition state theorists, mainly of those firms and the competition arising out of the attempts of nation states to either keep or further attract capital.

The main purpose of the competition state is hence to make societies fit for attracting capital and increase productivity in competition with others. This purpose follows from a supply-side logic: economy and society need to create the conditions for productivity and welfare to increase, which is supposed to happen through the different competitive strategies of two main types. On the one hand, states can try to manipulate a range of *domestic* variables in order to increase "internal" productivity, like deregulation of labour and product markets (Peters 2008), welfare state retrenchment (Kus 2006) and flexibilization (Ferrera & Rhodes 2000), boosting of national innovation systems (Nelson 1993) or the restructuring of domestic corporate governance (Porter 1990: 78). On the other hand, measures can also be employed to attract *foreign* investment and hence "import" capital and productivity, for example through lowering corporate tax rates (Avi-Yonah 2000), creating investment incentives for R&D (Cantwell & Mudambi 2000), liberalizing trade regimes (Bergsten 1996), attracting highly skilled migrants (Lavenex 2007) or "locking in" competition policies within supranational organizations such as the EU (Buch-Hansen & Wigger 2011). Taken together, both sets of measures describe the working logic of modern competition states.

---

3. For the key reference for this idea of international competitiveness of nations see Porter (1990).

If we look closely at the policy prescriptions states followed in the last three decades, the competition state thesis has some analytical and empirical purchase. Examples like the "third way" debate in the early 2000s illustrate attempts to navigate political tensions between global competitive pressures and the policy space left for governments (Giddens 2013). At the same time, the competition state thesis has been subject to much criticism over time. Its proponents often took globalization to be a deterministic concept, inevitably leading to the described competitive pressures; and they often described supply-side policies as the only perceivable answer to these pressures.[4] In short, while neoliberal globalization is real, there should, at least theoretically, be alternatives for states to deal with it than the competition state script. For a long time, however, these alternatives were rarely discernible in the practical reality of the global political economy.

I argue that transnational state investment represents such an alternative form of states dealing with the fact of neoliberal globalization. The phenomena described here and in the following chapters – states becoming global owners, the development of different strategies to capture financial returns, the sheer size of cross-border investment by states – are at odds with the idea that neoliberal globalization inevitably pressures states into the straitjacket of competition state politics. The unlikely successes of states like Singapore, Norway and Qatar as serious global owners indicate that state transformation could have entered a new phase, which is something that competition state explanations cannot sufficiently describe. Some of those countries were able to set up large SWFs with a global outreach that guaranteed a steady return on their financial investments; others reformed and mobilized massive SOEs to transnationalize and acquire strategic cross-border resources. The new role of transnational state capital suggests that neoliberal globalization does not only create downward pressures for states to adapt to, but also presents an opportunity for states to transform and expand state power and state capacity in the global system.

States with large natural or financial resources were hence able to move into the transnational agency space and compete with other economic actors within this space. Instead of succumbing entirely to the forces of neoliberal globalization, those states were able to instrumentalize these forces in order to reap the benefits of a globalized world economy. Recent academic literature has aimed to capture some of these trends via concepts like "state financialization" (Schwan *et al.* 2021) or the "shareholding state" (Wang 2015). In essence, these ideas aim to capture the fact that states are actively seeking to become parts of global financial and equity markets in a proactive manner. The shareholding

---

4. For a detailed discussion of these criticisms see Genschel and Seelkopf (2015).

Table 3.1 The competition state and competing state compared

State type	Competition state	Competing state
Working logic	*Indirect*: adapting to globalization	*Direct*: usage of transnational investment opportunities
Instruments	Domestic policies to improve competitiveness	Transnational instruments to reap benefits of globalization
Transnational agency space	*Constraining*: policy space shrinks for nation state	*Enabling*: investment of excess capital, oil revenues, forex reserves and acquisition of strategic targets
Geography	Potentially global (all states affected by globalization)	Global (transnational), but restricted to handful of powerful, resource-rich states

state, for example, comes close to the idea of the competing state: Wang (2015) describes how the Chinese state created state asset management bodies and investment vehicles in order to engage in proactive investment strategies.

This book takes this tendency in the literature a step further and beyond China only. States reinvented themselves as economic owners and developed different strategies for coping with globalization: instead of competing *passively* for global investment, they now compete *actively* on global markets as economic actors. The entirety of the strategies and tools states developed to do so – which are also dealt with in this book – make up the analytical figure of the *competing state*. Table 3.1 compares it with the state form of the competition state that was predominant during the heyday of neoliberal globalization in the 1990s and 2000s.

This contrast of both state forms is ideal-typical, which means that we will not find either of both in its pure form in the real world. In fact, the working logics of both state forms can sometimes go hand in hand, for example when a competing state engages in domestic structural reforms to also attract foreign investment. However, the contrast of both concepts illustrates the fundamentally different ways in which states can deal with globalization. Since the competition state literature almost exclusively dealt with the downwards pressures leading to domestic adaptation, the competing state perspective is an important corrective in this respect. It emphasizes the proactive and agency-related side of state power under neoliberal globalization and the opportunities arising out of it. The focus here is especially on the cross-border nature of these opportunities and the state strategies associated with realizing them.

The two largest states as owners, China and Norway, exemplify the ideal-typical strategies the competing state can adopt. The Norwegian model is one of a highly diversified global portfolio investor with a low risk profile. The Norwegian SWF draws on excess revenues from oil manufacturing which are then employed to create a steady return on investment, similar to other institutional investors. The Chinese foreign investment strategy is more comprehensive, with a mixture of SWF and strategic investment. Overall, the high propensity of Chinese investment to result in cross-border majority ownership is much more geostrategic than the Norwegian one, as the recent acquisitions of high-profile targets such as Syngenta illustrate. Both ideal-typical strategies demonstrate how states are able to enter and use the transnational agency space: the Norwegian strategy uses its ability to invest in globalized financial and equity markets, while the Chinese strategy profits from the opportunity to acquire specialized knowledge and technological assets through cross-border M&As. The list of state strategies as global investors is extended in Chapters 4 and 5 to types like the Russian state, which uses state capital investment in order to realize its geopolitical goals; or to fundamentally different strategies like the Singaporean one, which is interested in preserving the city state's tight integration in global production and capital networks.

An important characteristic differentiating the competing from the competition state is that not every state can become one. As I detail in the following, over 150 states have built up transnational investment connections as of the end of the 2010s. Out of this vast pool of states, only some are especially successful and relevant as global owners. It is a handful of states that possess the ability to actually compete with other economic actors for gains in the global economy. They are typically resource-rich economies that employ those resources to partake in global investment. These resources have different origins, such as oil extraction revenues, massive foreign exchange reserves or other high-value revenue-generating commodities. The competing state is hence a very unequal state form. This has important implications for international politics: states that are able to bundle and transnationalize economic power influence and also disrupt other structures and patterns of international politics, such as climate change mitigation efforts or multilateral cooperation. Chapter 6 delves into these matters and excavates what the transformation of states into global owners means for different realms of international politics.

Today, many of those states are extremely successful in entering the global economy: at the beginning of 2020, the Norwegian SWF announced a 20 per cent return on its investments for the previous year, held over $1.1 billion in AuM and owned about 1.5 per cent of all globally listed stocks (CNBC 2020). Meanwhile, the Chinese takeover of Swiss Syngenta in 2017 was the largest Chinese foreign acquisition ever, while the Russian state-led Rosneft investment into Essar Oil (also in 2017) was the largest inwards investment ever recorded in India (Babic *et al.* 2020). These numbers make clear that the existence of transnational state capital is more than just a by-product of globalization, but it pertains to our understanding of the policy space and power of (some) states as owners that has been gained within the global political economy.

Measuring state capital: how do we know it when we see it?

The evolution of states into global owners, and their transformation into competing states, is not an abstract process. We can in fact fairly precisely measure where and how strong state capital is on the rise and which strategies states as owners employ to achieve this. Measuring phenomena in the social world is thereby not something that is only of relevance to social scientists. In public and political discussions, we often tend to speak about different issues under the header of one concept or term. This might not always be a problem, as different people or social groups might want to emphasize different aspects of an issue. At the same time, it can become an impasse or outright problem if we are not using a precise vocabulary. As we saw in Chapter 1, "state capitalism" is predestinated to become such a fuzzy, diffuse and controversial concept. The focus of this book on state capital disentangles these problems to a certain degree and creates a clearer focus on states as owners. But what does it exactly cover and how can we empirically trace state capital? This raises the question of measurement: how do we know state capital when we see it?

To begin with, I understand state capital as all the corporate ownership claims a state possesses. This means that every time a state has or takes an ownership stake of size X in a company, it controls Y amount of state capital. This stake can be nominally very little – think about the stake of 0.89 per cent of the Norwegian SWF in Amazon[5] – or amount to full ownership. In return, the owning state receives dividends and other economic rights derived from such an ownership claim in a (foreign) company. Figure 3.1 depicts this relation as ownership tie. Figure 3.2 disaggregates this ownership tie into the different relevant categories depending on the size of the ownership stake a state holds in a company. As mentioned in Chapter 1, the focus of this book is the cross-border dimension of state capital, so I focus on transnational ties exclusively.

An ownership tie alone is, however, not enough to determine the exact amount of capital a state controls through a tie. There is a difference between owning part of Apple or General Motors, and owning a stake in a medium-sized automotive supply business from southern Germany. In order to account for this difference, I take into account the firm size when calculating the weight of the ownership tie. The amount of state capital that is controlled through a single ownership tie can then be simply calculated by multiplying the size of the ownership tie by the operating revenue of the target firm[6].

---

5. This was the case in January 2021. Source: Bureau van Dijk's ORBIS database.
6. For an extensive discussion of why operating revenue is the best-fitting measure for firm size in this case see Babic *et al.* (2020).

Figure 3.1 Transnational state ownership tie

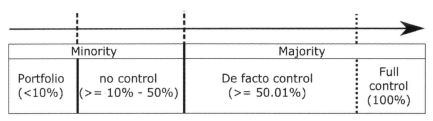

Figure 3.2 Different levels of a transnational ownership tie
Note: arrow represents tie.

Furthermore, I aggregate all these weighted ownership ties at the state level. This allows me to analyse *states* as owners – and not only particular state-owned vehicles. Such a methodological decision is strengthened by recent research doing exactly that.[7] There are, furthermore, two substantial reasons for not only looking at individual vehicles and firms but aggregating them at the state level. One is that state ownership is, despite all its variety, still closely tied to state power. As Brett Christophers puts it somewhat radically for national oil companies, "the national government *becomes* the company board" (Christophers 2021: 260, emphasis in original). Whereas the relative distance to state power certainly increases for other types of state capital, such as portfolio investment vehicles, it is still the case that states represent the ultimate owners of these vehicles and assets. Second, a large part of this book is concerned with the reverberations of the rise of states as global owners for international politics. For many governments and policy-makers, state-led investment is perceived with suspicion exactly because it is *state*-led. Whether or not state interests and state power play a role in cross-border investment, the concerns and hence international political consequences resulting from transnational state investment are often caused by this fact (see Babic & Dixon 2022; Cuervo-Cazurra 2018). In order to understand the international political reverberations of state-led investment, it is hence crucial to aggregate this investment at the state level for analytical reasons. In what follows, I build on

---

7. See, for example, Babic (2021); Babic *et al.* (2020); Carney (2018); Haberly and Wójcik (2017).

this idea when discussing state strategies in the global economy, where I refine this approach in the respective case studies.

In sum, we can observe transnational state capital when (1) a state invests money outside its own borders, (2) this investment leads to a certain degree of corporate control and (3) we can determine the value of this investment as described above. This methodological procedure allows us to actually "see" how states as global owners behave, what types of strategies they pursue and where these strategies end up. It allows us to study the phenomenon of state capital in a globalized world in an empirically rigorous manner. In this book, I build my analysis on these methodological considerations of how to measure state capital.

Seeing state capital: strategies, global trends and numbers

Now that we know how to see transnational state capital, it becomes possible to make statements about how it behaves in the global political economy. Generally speaking, states can adopt two different ideal-typical strategies when transnationalizing investment. For one, they can become owners of large capital resources and invest those in small percentages in all sorts of global asset classes. The strategic intent is to receive a good return on these investments, which typically involves a broad and diversified investment strategy. I call this a *financial* strategy. The ownership ties such a strategy creates mostly result in so-called portfolio stakes. These are small and usually non-controlling. In accordance with the United Nations Conference on Trade and Development (UNCTAD) definition, I set the threshold for portfolio investment below 10 per cent of all stakes of the invested company (see also Figure 3.2).[8] The diversification of investment makes such portfolio strategies less likely to be engaged in politically charged takeover battles. Rather, states that tend to invest most of their capital portfolio do so relatively unscathed. At the same time, those states can also build up large portfolio positions in the global economy – just think about Norway or other states with large SWFs that became powerful global actors mostly through portfolio investment.

On the other side of the strategic spectrum, we find what I call controlling strategies. States that tend to invest most of their capital in majority-owned or fully owned firms display such an inclination to control these firms. The strategic intent here is not so much to receive direct financial returns on investment, but rather to capture important assets, technologies or simply know-how from foreign firms. States like China have a strong interest

---

8. According to He *et al.* (2016: 188): "[t]he 10 per cent cutoff is high enough that the state likely influences corporate governance and thereby affects firm performance".

Table 3.2 Different transnational state investment strategies

		Ownership segment		
		<10%	*10–50%*	*>=50.01%*
Total amount of transnational state capital in this segment	*Total (>=90%)*	Financial (**F**)		Control (**C**)
	Absolute (<90%, but >= 50%)	Dominantly financial (**FD**)	Mixed (**M**)	Dominantly control (**CD**)
	<50%, but relative majority of state capital	Mixed financial (**MF**)		Mixed control (**MC**)

Note: The strategies are in the shaded box.

in acquiring such assets in the global economy, for example as part of its "Made in China 2025" (MiC) industrial development strategy (Jungbluth 2018). Acquiring whole firms gives those states the possibility to transfer such knowledge, or to consolidate their foothold in international markets. I set the threshold from where we can speak of a controlling strategy at 50.01 per cent of all shares of the invested firm. This conservatively high threshold allows me to incorporate only those cases in the strategic profile of a state that are clear-cut. Only when a state controls the absolute majority of shares in a firm, and only if a state tends to invest predominantly in such a way, can we speak of a clear controlling strategic interest. Naturally, these controlling strategies as exemplified by large owners such as Russia or France will play a central role in Chapter 6, where I discuss the geoeconomic consequences of states becoming (strategic) owners.

These two ideal-typical positions represent the two ends of a spectrum that can be further differentiated. Most of the competing states I find are located somewhere on this spectrum, and only a few are clear portfolio or control-ling strategies. Table 3.2 maps the different possible strategies. I combine two dimensions to determine a strategy. First, where is the majority of a state's transnational capital invested (in portfolio, controlling or in-between stakes) (*horizontal dimension*)? Second, how strong is this majority (simple majority, absolute majority or total (>90 per cent) majority) (*vertical dimension*)? The intersection of both dimensions determines a state's strategy. Such an approach has the benefit of being both exhaustive (it covers the entire horizontal and vertical dimensions) and mutually exclusive (each state can be allocated only one specific strategy on the spectrum described in Table 3.2).

With these measurement and conceptual considerations in mind, we can start making sense of – or simply "see" – the state as an owner in the global political economy. In a first step, we can have a look at the overall numbers distributed by ownership segment (Figure 3.3)

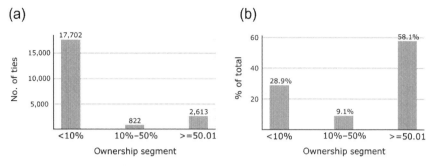

Figure 3.3 Distribution of state ownership ties (a) and state capital (b) across different ownership segments

The comparison of the two distributions reveals that most ties are located in the portfolio segment, while most state capital is concentrated in majority ownership. This might not be entirely surprising, as a higher ownership stake (as is the case for majority ownership) translates to a higher total amount of state capital following the measure applied in this book. Another relevant point is that the creation of a portfolio ownership tie is in theory much easier than owning whole firms cross-border. State investment through small ownership stakes is a much more liquid[9] form of investment than the acquisition of foreign firms, or of the internationalization of domestic firms ending up in majority ownership. The high number of portfolio ties and the correspondingly lower number of high-value majority ties reinforces the point I made earlier about the fact that not every state can become a competing state. In order to invest significant amounts of capital abroad, states need to own abundant resources and have the organizational ability to conduct these large-scale projects. The distributions displayed in Figure 3.3 illustrate this on a global scale.

When we aggregate the weighted cross-border ownership ties at the state level, we can see which states are the largest transnational owners of foreign state investment (Table 3.3). What is remarkable about this distribution is the diversity of states at the top. States as different as China, Norway, Singapore, the United Arab Emirates (UAE) and France top the list. All of these states and their cross-border investment activities stem from different economic circumstances. Some owners, like France, have a long tradition of national industrial "champions" which received strong state support over decades and are now entering foreign markets (such as EDF) (see also Coutant 2014). Others, like

---

9. Liquidity of assets is defined as the potential of these assets to be converted into cash. For our purposes, it is important that stocks and shareholdings below majority ownership are more liquid than the ownership of whole firms. This means that the investment through financial strategies is, *ceteris paribus*, more liquid than that of controlling strategies.

Table 3.3 The ten largest states as owners

State	State capital outflow (billion US$)
China	385
Norway	310
Singapore	115
UAE	110
France	101
Russia	87
Sweden	73
Canada	56
Saudi Arabia	53
Qatar	49
Kuwait	43

Source: own calculations based on ORBIS data.

the UAE, only recently managed to transform their oil wealth into worldwide corporate shareholdings by setting up successful SWFs. Again, others like China integrated state capital transnationalization in its monumental catch-up development strategy to become one of the largest global owners (see also Shambaugh 2013). The emergence of the competing state is hence a global, variegated phenomenon: different states as owners internationalize state capital in the search for returns on investment, the acquisition of assets or the drive for economic catch-up. At the same time, state capital is globally quite concentrated: the top 20 states as owners control more than 90 per cent of all globally invested state capital. Each of the top 20 owns at least 1 per cent of the total global amount.

There are hence different historical and economic circumstances on the basis of which states become global owners. At the same time, they are part of the same global economy, and they aim to reap the opportunities of this global economy through different strategies. In short, they compete with other economic actors for relative gains. The strategies the largest states as owners employ are listed in Table 3.4.

It is clear that only a few of the largest states as owners really pursue original financial strategies. States like Norway or Canada are an exception here – however, globally speaking, we can find more financial strategies than controlling ones. Again, this has to do with the fact that it is theoretically easier to invest in small, non-controlling stakes outside a state's borders than to steer massive amounts of state capital in the global economy. Mixed cases like Singapore or Qatar are interesting, since they suggest that states can opt to pursue state capital transnationalization via various channels at the same time. Qatar, for example, employs a mixture of oil-related majority investment in combination with a selective but broad strategy of targeted portfolio investment in listed firms,

Table 3.4 The strategic profiles of the ten largest states as owners

State	Strategy
China	Control (*CD*)
Norway	Financial (*F*)
Singapore	Mixed (*MC*)
UAE	Control (*CD*)
France	Control (*CD*)
Russia	Control (*CD*)
Sweden	Control (*CD*)
Canada	Financial (*F*)
Saudi Arabia	Control (*CD*)
Qatar	Mixed (*M*)
Kuwait	Control (*CD*)

high-end real estate and other high-value assets. Singapore, as we will see in Chapter 5, is another unique state as owner that in many ways has perfected the exploitation of the transnational agency space of neoliberal globalization in the last two decades.

Whereas foreign state-led investment stems from a limited number of powerful states, it flows into almost every region of the world. Table 3.5 shows the targets of state capital by macro world regions[10].

The different European regions are by far the most attractive investment targets. Taken together, they make up almost half of all global foreign state-led investment. All European regions also have a positive ratio between controlling and portfolio investment. This indicates that the state capital flowing into these regions is more strategic than in other regions: the invested states own on average majority stakes in their invested firms, which is usually a long-term, high-capital-intensive commitment compared to the more liquid portfolio investment. In addition to this ratio, the European regions also tend to have relatively low Gini coefficients. This means that the states invested in these regions do so on a comparable level. In other words, the inequality between the investors is lower than in other cases (for example in the Asian regions). Taken together, state-led investment is a global phenomenon with a strategic focus on Europe as a target. The reasons for this focus certainly lie in the fact that Europe is home to many successful industrial champions that represent attractive investment targets, especially for more controlling strategies. As an

---

10. I used the M49 standard of the UN geoscheme ("standard country or area codes for statistical use", see UNSD 2019) to code the targets of foreign state-led investment. Some of the regions were too small to be an investment target, so I merged them in the following way with larger regions: Melanesia and Micronesia were merged with South East Asia, and Polynesia was merged with Australia and New Zealand.

Table 3.5 The targets of foreign state-led investment by geographical region

Area	Inflow (billion US$ and % of total)	Control–portfolio ratio	Gini coefficient
Western Europe	379 (21.8%)	5.1	0.51
North America	284 (16.3%)	0.1	0.76
Northern Europe	259 (14.9%)	2.4	0.68
South-East Asia	234 (13.4%)	33.7	0.82
Southern Europe	157 (9%)	13.7	0.68
East Asia	133 (7.6%)	0.2	0.73
Australia and New Zealand	111 (6.4%)	10.6	0.71
Latin America and the Caribbean	62 (3.6%)	2.9	0.75
Eastern Europe	36 (2.1%)	3.2	0.68
South Asia	34 (2%)	1.6	0.74
West Asia	34 (1.9%)	4.1	0.76
Sub-Saharan Africa	11 (0.7%)	0.4	0.73
North Africa	5 (0.3%)	13.5	0.77
Central Asia	2 (0.1 %)	1254.8	0.78

Note: a control-portfolio ratio above 1 indicates higher volumes of majority ownership in the region; a ratio below 1 indicates a majority of portfolio investment. The Gini coefficient indicates the degree of investment inequality in a region (the higher the coefficient, the more unequal are the invested states as owners).

example, the Chinese industrial catch-up strategy MiC aims to make China a world leader in ten global key industries by 2025. Germany, Austria and other states in western Europe have been targeted by Chinese SOEs and other vehicles in this endeavour, with some success in taking over important niche industrial firms in recent years (Jungbluth 2018; Wübbeke *et al.* 2016).

In sum, it becomes clear that there is a limited number of forms states can adopt when transnationalizing state capital. At the same time, many of these different forms are present among the largest states as owners, which indicates that state capital is a variegated phenomenon. There is no "best practice" or single way of competing for economic gains in the global political economy. The following chapters add more qualitative insights to this argument: even when states apply similar strategies, the motivations and targets of these strategies will most likely differ on the ground. This "polymorphism" (see Alami & Dixon 2020a) of state capital transnationalization illustrates the usefulness of the concept of the competing state: it captures the fact that states use state capital transnationalization for a variety of reasons but in a limited number of forms. States as owners compete for various goals such as returns on investment, or the acquisition of key technologies and assets in the global economy through a limited number of forms and strategies. The competing state idea summarizes this phenomenon and leaves room to define more accurately the respective idiosyncratic strategies of different states as owners.

This general overview gives us an idea of how states transnationalize their capital, and which states as owners are successful in doing so. From this bird's-eye perspective, we can survey and neatly sort the world of the competing state. Quantitatively oriented political economy studies can use such a perspective to test, compare and draw valuable conclusions analysing the relationships between different characteristics of the competing state and other variables. At the same time, this general perspective alone remains unsatisfactory. What are the motivations, strategies, dynamics and effects of states as global owners? How do different states attempt to realize their strategies and how does this affect international relations in turn? The quantitative study of state capital alone will not answer these questions. In order to amend this, we need to zoom in on particular cases and strategies and closely study their effects "on the ground". In other words, the described phenomena need to be brought to life. I do so in the remainder of this book. Chapters 4 and 5 closely examine the strategic choices of particular states as owners, while Chapter 6 scrutinizes the various consequences of the rise of transnational state capital.

One alternative way of choosing the analysed cases in the following would be to simply pick the largest states as owners as described above. This would, however, not serve the goal of describing the variety of current foreign state investment in the global political economy. A better alternative is to pick different typical representatives of particular strategies, and to cover a broader spectrum of existing state capital transnationalization strategies. In the following two chapters, I pick cases that fall into one of the two identified ideal-typical camps of controlling and financial strategies.

Chapter 4 deals with the controlling strategies of China, Russia and Germany and France, which are discussed together. China is the largest and most powerful competing state in the current global political economy and hence also displays a very idiosyncratic transnationalization strategy. Russia is in many ways a classical geopolitical actor regarding the question of foreign state-led investment, as its large state-owned fossil fuel firms illustrate. However, a less well-known fact is that Russian state-owned financial capital also plays an increasingly important role in its cross-border investment strategy. The cases of Germany and France are relevant because both are rather unlikely "state capitalists" when we look into the literature on the topic. Both are nevertheless major owners of transportation and logistics firms cross-border, which puts both in important positions regarding the ownership and control of the logistical nodes of European capitalism.

Chapter 5 scrutinizes the financial strategies of Norway as the most prominent and powerful example of this type of state as owner. The Norwegian story is particularly insightful for many of the core questions raised with regards to transnational state capital and which are dealt with in Chapter 6. The second case I discuss in Chapter 5 is Singapore and its strategic choices. Singapore is a relevant case not only because it wields enormous weight in the global economy despite being a small state. It also owns and steers two different sovereign funds with different mandates and functions that enable the state to pursue a mixed strategy incorporating elements of both the financial and controlling strategies.

4

Strategies of the competing state: controlling strategies

This chapter deals with what I described in Chapter 3 as the "controlling" strategies of states as global owners. By controlling strategy I refer to the fact that the vast majority of the transnational ownership ties created by these states are located in majority- or full-ownership stakes. Since the amount of ownership correlates, *ceteris paribus*, with the corporate control a shareholder has over the invested firm,[1] such strategies are more likely to grant the owning state control over its cross-border invested firms. All the cases discussed in this chapter embrace one variety of such a controlling strategy. At the same time, all cases are also distinct regarding their background, intent, scope and effects, among other things. What looks like the same strategy from a distance is quite distinct in close-up.

China's quest for economic dominance

China is not only the largest among all states as owners but also the most prominent example of statist practices in the global political economy. The rise of China as global economic powerhouse since the 1980s is inextricably linked to the role of state-owned and state-directed economic vehicles, be it large or small, national or local SOEs, investment funds or its development banks. Starting in 1978, the government under Deng Xiaoping introduced sweeping reforms that dynamized the inert, centrally planned Chinese economy. Besides "opening up" China for foreign investment, the reform of state ownership

---

1. For a discussion of this issue see La Porta *et al.* (1999).

became a central issue. If the Chinese political economy was to become globally competitive, its massive state sector had to adapt one way or another.

The advent of neoliberal globalization introduced another opportunity, but also a point of pressure for the transforming state-directed Chinese economy. Global competition for FDI attraction and the capture of parts of transnationally integrated value chains began to take shape in the late 1980s.[2] A large, inefficient and inaccessible state sector was generally seen as an obstacle to survive and thrive as an economy in such a world. In Washington and elsewhere, recipes for developing economies to become "competitive" through deregulation and liberalization were cooked up (Williamson 1990). Many countries in Latin America, East Asia and the former Soviet Union became subject to what has been dubbed the neoliberal "shock doctrine" (Klein 2007): the fast and hard introduction of market-oriented reforms that often resulted in heightened inequality and deep structural problems. The curious point about the Chinese experience is that it managed to "escape shock therapy" (Weber 2021) through a gradualism that managed to reform without giving up state control.

With this gradualism, the Chinese state leadership successfully navigated the first two decades of its secular transformation programme. For state ownership reforms, this meant a trial-and-error programme that allowed it to successively reduce state ownership while concentrating economic resources and political power in a number of large SOEs towards the end of the 1990s (Li & Cheong 2019). One of the main reforms in this period was the creation of the State-owned Assets Supervision and Administration Commission (SASAC) in 2003. SASAC acts as a type of supervisory and management body for around 100 centrally owned large SOEs. The body was created in the first instance to reduce state ownership in the Chinese economy. At the same time, a nominal reduction of state ownership under SASAC also meant a modernization and streamlining of large SOEs that had been inefficient and inert giants under the auspices of bureaucratic ministries. The cutback on redundancies and the standardization of outdated corporate governance systems led to a concentration of economic power under SASAC. As a result, the reforms nominally reduced, but *de facto* increased, the grip and agency of the Chinese state as an owner.

SASAC and further reforms were elements in the larger "going-out" strategy that was developed by the government at the turn of the millennium. Together with China's entrance into the WTO in 2001, the government aimed to increase the presence of Chinese investment in the world economy. During this phase, the direct state control of outgoing Chinese investment was flanked

---

2. See, for example, Linsi (2020) for the changing FDI regimes of the UK and other major economies at the time.

by state assistance for other, non-state-owned firms. The going-out strategy took off in the early 2000s, with a tenfold increase of yearly outwards investment numbers by the end of the decade (Shambaugh 2013: 141). State-led investment was always a part of this dynamic: first, as only a select number of SOEs were even engaged in meaningful outwards investment in the 1990s; then, as national oil companies (NOCs) conducted large-scale outward investment in the 2000s; and finally, as record-breaking cross-border deals by large SOEs like ChemChina or State Grid aimed at securing critical technologies and know-how in the global economy in the 2010s.

This development reflects the rise of the competing state form: the Chinese state evolved from incrementally engaging with the global political economy with carefully selected SOEs, to offensively capturing assets and lead firms in globally competitive sectors such as agrochemicals or robotics. The evolution of the competing state thereby follows closely the different phases of the general going-out strategy of Beijing and even its five-year plans (Shambaugh 2013: 140). In other words, the incremental changes we see in the relation between state-owned Chinese capital and the global political economy are of a strategic nature. The function that the Chinese state as global owner assumes today is embedded in a broader strategy of China to transition from the "workshop of the world" to a knowledge economy. This strategic nature is also reflected in its controlling ownership profile.

Syngenta: the deal that shook the (agrochemical) world

In May 2017, Erik Fyrwald had a lot to explain to an astounded financial press. He had just become the CEO of one of China's largest state-owned multinational companies, when ChemChina invested over $40 billion to take over agrochemical giant Syngenta. Fyrwald, the old and new CEO of the Switzerland-based firm, felt the need to emphasize that "[i]t is very important to understand that this is a financial transaction" (cited in Shields 2017). Of course, it was much more than that: it was the largest outwards investment ever made by China (private or state owned); it meant the takeover of one of the leading agrochemical firms in the world, rattling the industry; and it delivered the Chinese state a competitive edge in important agrochemical techniques. In 2020, a merger between ChemChina and the other large state-owned firm Sinochem marked the creation of the largest chemical corporation in the world. Besides Syngenta, other world-leading subsidiaries like Israeli pesticide producer Adama belong to the newly formed Chinese state-owned agrochemical empire.

This episode combines a number of characteristics of the Chinese competing state. ChemChina acquired a producer of high-end goods in the global agrochemical business, which will increase the safety and reliability of China's domestic food production. The deal also made the Chinese SOE a central player in the globally competitive seeds business overnight. Furthermore, the new owners delisted Syngenta from the stock exchange, which concentrated ownership and control entirely in the hands of ChemChina. Finally, the merger with Sinochem was only the latest in a series of takeovers of smaller competitors like Brazilian Strider, UK-based Floranova and Italian Valagro. All of those aspects – the acquisition of leading technologies, the competition for global market shares, the exercise of full control over acquired companies and the further global consolidation within the industry – exemplify China's strategic outlook with regards to state capital transnationalization. The Syngenta takeover in 2017 hence strikingly illustrates the Chinese outwards investment strategy.

Taking on the world

The strategic behaviour of the Chinese state as owner does, however, vary across industries and regions. The Syngenta case attracted global attention because of its sheer size. Other acquisitions have tended to go on under the radar of public scrutiny, at least for a while. They also often do not involve the whole repertoire of takeover, control, delisting and consolidation. The takeover and delisting of Italian tyre manufacturer Pirelli in 2015 was, for example, followed by a relisting and reduction of ChemChina's shares to below 50 per cent in 2017. Other less attention-grabbing projects were the many takeovers of German industrial enterprises that are global market leaders in their respective niches such as Kiekert (automobile parts, 2012), KraussMaffei (industrial engineering, 2016) or EEW (waste incineration, 2017). The discussion about these cases gained traction when the German government blocked a planned takeover of electricity network provider 50Hertz by the SASAC company State Grid in 2018 for reasons of national security. In other cases, as in many Latin American or African countries, Chinese state-led investment is focused on energy production and logistical hubs, such as the acquisition of a major Brazilian port in Sao Luis in 2019. Put simply, the Chinese investment strategy with its global grip on a variety of high-value assets is the prime example of how the competing state of the twenty-first century is able to exploit the transnational agency space created by neoliberal globalization.

An examination of the global spread of Chinese state-led investment shows the truly global dimension of the Chinese strategy. China is invested in 66 other countries around the world, from Australia to Italy, from Kazakhstan to Mexico. It is invested in every single global region of the UN geoscheme.[3] Similarly, the variety of invested industries ranges from "classical" sites of state investment, such as manufacturing and mining, to others like agriculture, transportation and logistics, construction and financial corporations. It is furthermore present in the main geoindustrial clusters with potential for state-led geoeconomic competition and plays a major role in many of those clusters (Babic 2021). This globality is a major feature of China's foreign investment strategy. There is no comparable state as owner that invests such large amounts of capital in such a diversified and global manner. Other large-scale owners like Norway or the UAE are also globally diversified, but often own "only" small portfolio stakes in large publicly listed companies. Other owners – like Russia – also own large assets outside their own borders but lack the geographical spread of China's profile and are focused on European investment targets. This unique combination of the sheer size, geographical spread and diversity of investments makes China the *primus inter pares* of states as global owners. The discussion of the consequences of the rise of transnational state capital for international politics in Chapter 6 of this book comes back to the power that China yields from this unique position.

MiC and what is the Chinese state?

This growth of China as a large and powerful global owner is not taking place in a vacuum. The large-scale acquisitions of leading firms in global industries, of important nodes in global value chains and of so-called "hidden champions" in the small and medium-sized enterprise (SME) segment fits into the broader Chinese industrial strategy. A large part of that strategy is often identified as the official MiC agenda. MiC is an industrial policy programme that aims at transforming the Chinese economy into a globally leading high-tech manufacturing hub by 2025. Officially begun in 2015, the Chinese leadership set out a plan to "move up" the proverbial value chain in ten key industries, from IT to aerospace and aviation, and from "green" electric equipment to biomedicine and agriculture (State Council 2017). A key element of this strategic project is to leverage the various economic powers of the Chinese state to propel this transformation directly and indirectly. Besides well-known industrial policy tools like subsidizing exports of high-end goods and other domestic market

---

3. The UN geoscheme includes 14 world regions, see: https://unstats.un.org/unsd/methodol ogy/m49.

interventions, the Chinese state also engages in acquiring advanced technologies and knowledge in foreign markets (Wübbeke *et al.* 2016). In fact, the patterns of Chinese takeovers in cases like Germany over recent years suggest that these acquisitions are clearly aimed at the ten sectors covered in the MiC proposal (Jungbluth 2018).

Acquiring foreign technologies through state support is thus a key objective of the broader MiC plan. While this strategy is not reducible to the role of foreign state investment, it still plays a paramount role for MiC. Cases like the Syngenta takeover fit neatly into MiC, as cutting-edge agrochemical technology, and with it the "higher" ends of global value chains, are captured. The strategic acquisition of foreign technologies and assets through state investment is hence part and parcel of the broader Chinese going-out strategy, and concretely of MiC. In other words, the Chinese competing state uses the transnational agency space created by neoliberal globalization to realize its strategic goals. This outwards orientation also arguably entails a domestic component: by reaching beyond its borders to capture relevant assets, China aims to develop domestic manufacturing and other industrial processes and make them smart, green and lean. This applies in cases like the Syngenta deal that is supposed to raise domestic agricultural quality and output (Patton 2018), as well as to the systematic buying up of niche German SMEs to make China a leading technological power. The "transnational" strategies of the Chinese competing state are hence crucially intertwined with its domestic development model.

The role of state-led investment and asset and technology capture for the MiC strategy raises the question of how we should understand state power in this context. After all, if the Chinese competing state strategies are well aligned with its MiC and broader development goals, one could assume that the Chinese state is a well-functioning, highly centralized actor that moves its political as well as economic pieces over the chessboard of international politics. Indeed, political discussions in the West are often shaped by such an image. However, as a growing body of research has shown, the Chinese state can hardly be conceptualized as such a unitary actor in the global political economy.[4] Rather, the overseas engagement of various state-owned or state-affiliated Chinese actors is better described as fragmented and incoherent, which limits the likelihood of them being employed as "tools" of economic statecraft abroad. This fragmentation can also be explained by the nature of the transnational agency space of the global economy: this space facilitates and enables certain types of transnational outreach (such as foreign investment or

---

4. See Hameiri and Jones (2016, 2021). For transnationally active Chinese SOEs see Jones and Zou (2017), and for Chinese oil elites see de Graaff (2020).

trade) but does not do so for others (such as regulatory outreach or the extension of specific political authority into global markets). Consequently, the rise of states in the global political economy remains necessarily fragmented to a certain degree.

Such an understanding also applies to the issue of Chinese foreign state investment and the state's grip on this investment. As discussed in the previous chapters, I regard a state's investment strategy rather as an imperfect pattern than the one-to-one empirical realization of a grand (investment) strategy. At the same time, and in the case of controlling strategies like the Chinese one, these patterns can give us an indication about the nature and intent of investment strategies that need to be complemented by qualitative empirical evidence. In the case of China and MiC, this evidence of a correlation between the targets of Chinese foreign state investment and specific sectors is discussed above. Hence, while we should assume that by nature the transnationalization of Chinese state capital is a fragmented, incoherent process, the fact that its emerging patterns overlap with official strategic development goals (such as noted in the MiC strategy) indicates at least attempts at coordination in the Chinese outwards strategy. This coordination achievement also suggests that Chinese state power and control over its foreign state investment strategy is more advanced and integrated than we would assume in other controlling strategies without such strategic overlap. Such a view represents a middle ground between a mostly unsubstantiated belief in a unitary Chinese state in full control and the agnostic position that we cannot say anything meaningful about the Chinese outwards investment strategy (see also Hameiri & Jones 2021).

A changing Chinese strategy in a protectionist world

What is the future of the Chinese outwards strategy? The success of this strategy, especially in the second decade of the twenty-first century, in capturing major assets, technologies and knowledge was also a product of an open global economy. The rise of China as economic superpower was only possible in a transnational agency space that allowed Chinese capital to enter other jurisdictions and that put up comparatively few obstacles for (Chinese) foreign state-led investment. This world is changing. Increasing protectionism and economic nationalism, ranging from softer forms of investment screening mechanisms to harder forms of direct state intervention, have been sweeping the globe in recent years. The rise of China in the global political economy is not the only reason for a hardening stance of many states around the world, but it is among the major reasons for such pervasive change. From this angle, a more protectionist global economy might cut short the Chinese competing state before it really takes off. An obvious example is the rise of investment screening mechanisms in Europe and elsewhere (Bauerle Danzman & Meunier 2021), which constitutes a direct closure of parts of the transnational agency space which Chinese state capital skilfully exploited before.

Such developments are not unlikely, and we may well see further closures of especially European and the US economies to Chinese investment, for all kinds of geoeconomic and protectionist reasons. Yet, thinking that this would mean an automatic end to the Chinese competing state underestimates the larger strategic changes taking place within the Chinese political economy. In the last decade, the large-scale acquisitions of different large and small enterprises with know-how, critical assets or technologies have helped to boost Chinese domestic development. The vast majority of these deals were mergers and takeovers: so-called brownfield investment in foreign corporations. The countermeasures that especially European states and the USA implemented to protect national infrastructure and key technologies from such takeovers, such as investment screening mechanisms, target precisely such brownfield investment. This is different for so-called greenfield investment, which covers new start-up projects realized abroad, and is thus often not considered problematic in the context of investment screening.[5] The reason for this seems straightforward: if a foreign company creates a new subsidiary or other productive facility, it benefits the domestic economy without the immediate accompanying risk of technology or asset transfer.

A stronger focus on greenfield investment could thus help the Chinese competing state to remain active in the global economy. China still holds comparatively little FDI stock in places like Europe: at the end of 2018, it held 2.8 per cent compared to 25.1 per cent of the USA or 18.9 per cent of the UK (Eurostat). A similar picture emerges for the USA. This is far from a critical threshold, but rather indicates that Chinese (state-led) investment still has enough room to manoeuver in the global economy. A stronger focus on greenfield investment could in the long run even turn out to be beneficial for the Chinese competing state: different from M&As, greenfield investment theoretically gives investors more control to develop their investment from scratch, and the investor does not usually encounter resistance and existing (management) structures as is the case with takeovers. Both points are well aligned with the Chinese outwards strategy of controlling its overseas investment. In 2020, this tendency was already visible, with a survey among Chinese investors in the

---

5. This is, for example, the case in Germany (see BMWi 2019) and for most greenfield transactions into the USA under the Committee on Foreign Investment in the United States.

USA suggesting that a majority of the signed deals was indeed for greenfield investment (CGCC 2020: 6).

Moving away from large-scale takeovers and M&As could help to appease the critical voices in the EU and the USA that accuse the Chinese of pursuing a strategy of asset and technology transfer, and thereby salvage the Chinese competing state for the future. A frequently mentioned point in these discussions is the lack of reciprocity of economic relations between China and other industrialized states. Whereas the EU in particular was for a long time relatively open to Chinese (state-led) investment, market access in China was less straightforward for European firms. At the end of 2020, the Comprehensive Agreement on Investment (CAI) between China and the EU was concluded after seven years of negotiation. The CAI is supposed to enhance and increase investment opportunities for both sides, and thus to contribute to higher levels of reciprocity. Whether or not this will be achieved with the CAI, the new emphasis on greenfield investment as well as the fact that China became the largest FDI recipient in 2020 (Reuters 2021) indicate that the Chinese competing state could transform substantially in the following decade. Rather than being outmanoeuvred by stricter investment screening and rising protectionism in the West, the Chinese competing state could prove to be more resilient and resourceful than its current strategy suggests. The Chinese quest for global economic dominance could enter a new phase, in which asset acquisition and technology transfer wane and the establishing and consolidation of Chinese (state-owned) companies in foreign markets becomes the new rationale. As we have seen, this can be accomplished despite rising protectionist tendencies around the world.

Russia: geopolitics in a globalized world

Russia is the best example of a geopolitical competing state. As the successor state of the Soviet Union, the Russian Federation inherited both a large state-owned economy as well as the economic problems of the late empire. Facing an unprecedented economic contraction in the early 1990s, the new Russian state opted for large-scale privatizations and market reforms. By the middle of the decade, 70 per cent of the economy was privatized and the government had initiated the infamous "loans for shares scheme" which sold major state-owned assets cheaply, especially in the energy sector (Shleifer & Treisman 2005: 153). In addition, the low oil and gas prices of the late 1980s did not recover through the 1990s, which cut a major source of income for the Russian state. High inflation added to this general malaise, and although growth showed signs of recovery at the end of the decade, Russian state capacity remained at low levels. The selling off of some of its major assets in the state-owned oil and gas industry reduced the state's grip on important strategic tools and revenue sources. The only major assets left in state hands were oil producer Rosneft and a blockholding position in gas producer Gazprom (Newnham 2011: 137). Different from the Chinese case, the Russian experience of the 1990s was almost entirely a domestic struggle to bring an economy in transition back on track, while a comprehensive strategy to build up competing state resources was not a real option.

This changed in the early 2000s for two reasons. First, politically, the new strongman Putin started early on to centralize power within the Kremlin, for example with a constitutional reform curtailing the powers of the regions and by rebalancing economic state power vis-à-vis oligarchs (Mommen 2004: 134). Crucially, Putin's reconfiguration of the political power structure of the Russian state at the time also involved renationalizing assets from mainly gas and oil firms (Hanson 2007). Second, the first decade of the new century experienced a commodity boom, with global oil prices rising almost exponentially and reaching record prices until shortly before the GFC of 2008. The Russian state-led and carbon-driven economy rode this wave of ever-rising prices and was able to pay off Russia's foreign debt that had put a strain on state power in the 1990s (Newnham 2011: 137). This increased state capacity massively, including with regards to foreign economic policy goals. At the end of the decade, Russia had transformed into a "Petrostate", whose foreign policy ambitions were backed by massive state-owned oil and gas assets (Goldman 2010).

The main "tools" of the Russian competing state are consequently its state-owned gas and oil companies like Rosneft (oil) and Gazprom (gas). Putin's government actively sought to "recapture" major players in the industry that had been sold off cheaply in the privatization waves of the 1990s. In the well-known Yukos case, the company was broken up and sold to state-owned Rosneft in 2004. In 2005, state-owned Gazprom acquired Sibneft, another major player in the Russian and European gas business, in a more conventional market transaction (Newnham 2011: 138). These and other instances of capture and acquisition of energy companies through the state laid the foundation for a more central role of those companies for Russian foreign economic policy. Such moves to concentrate state ownership at the central government level resemble the Chinese attempts to streamline and concentrate state ownership under SASAC in a similar time period. However, the Russian government had first to capture these firms and assets that had been privatized in the previous decade, which made the process much more politically contested and incurred a strong societal backlash.

Once under state control, the large energy firms were employed abroad, especially within Russia's neighbourhood. The Russian petro-companies could thereby rely on gas and oil pipelines and other ties to western Europe established during the Cold War. The launch of Russian outwards FDI began around the turn of the millennium and reached its peak just before the GFC, growing

17 times in value during that period (Andreff 2015). The expansion of its state-owned champions played a crucial role in this: firms like Gazprom established hundreds of subsidiaries and ownership stakes in and beyond Europe during these years, thereby extending the energy ties and the energy interdependencies between Russia and the EU. In strategy papers, Russian authorities repeatedly made it clear that resource-extracting firms in particular are tools of Russian cross-border statecraft as well as enjoying special protection via the state from foreign competition (Grätz 2014: 94). This strategic aspect "on paper" is reflected in the practice of those firms that are regularly part of geopolitical disputes, especially within Europe (Abdelal 2015). In the latest reiteration, Russian state-owned fossil fuel firms and their executives were at the heart of strong economic sanctions after the Putin government waged war on Ukraine in early 2022.

One of the main objectives of targeting Russian (transnational) state capital through sanctions is its support function for upholding the Russian regime in the long run: (state) ownership of especially fossil fuel assets is an integral part of Putin's power system (see, e.g., Djankov 2015). It is used for generating legitimacy among domestic elites through revenue sharing, and as a foreign policy tool such as that observed in the war on Ukraine. Western discussions about further tightening the screws on Russian sanctions in the spring of 2022 consequently circled around splintering the relation between Russia's state-controlled fossil fuel sector and the Putin regime. Despite these efforts, it is clear that years of European dependency on Russia for fossil fuel imports allowed these state-owned firms to thrive through cross-border investment. Furthermore, beyond just trade activities, firms like Gazprom created foreign subsidiaries and cross-border joint ventures, which strengthened the grip of Russian state capital on European energy markets. The key role such dependencies play in the current war on Ukraine and the difficulties of breaking them amid historical sanctions and the assault on a sovereign European country (Ukraine) exemplify the geopolitical nature of these ties. In a much stronger sense than in other cases of controlling strategies, the Russian competing state hence displays an instrumental attitude towards its state-owned energy firms investing cross-border. This is not only visible in the various "gas crises" in Russia's European vicinity in recent decades, and the war waged on Ukraine, but also in other cases around the world.

Rosneft, or what are geopolitics?

In the autumn of 2016, a gathering between the chairman of Rosneft, Igor Sechin, and the Ruia brothers, owners of Indian oil giant Essar Oil, took place on Mauritius (Zhdannikov *et al.* 2016). The reason for this meeting was to finalize a large-scale takeover of Essar Oil by Rosneft that had been in the making for some time. The successful acquisition was announced a month later during a meeting between Russian President Putin and Indian Prime Minister Modi at the BRICS meeting in Goa, India. The deal had historical dimensions: the $13 billion takeover was both the largest Russian outwards investment and the largest Indian inwards investment ever recorded. The deal seemed like a clear win–win situation for both governments: a show of force for Russian state-owned Rosneft, as well as a signalling of global competitiveness for the Indian oil industry.

However, the deal's circumstances soon turned out to be problematic. In 2017, Indian security agencies raised red flags over specific parts of the overall deal, which included the Vadinar port in the Indian state of Gujarat (Asian Age 2017). Rosneft would take control of a port which is in close proximity to Pakistan and thus a potential geostrategic asset. Essar and Rosneft, however, received the government concessions to proceed with the acquisition soon afterwards, and the deal was completed, despite the security concerns. In the end, Rosneft gained an important foothold in a growing Asian oil market and continued to extend its presence in global refining further. Russia is still a high-volume producer of crude oil, which makes the state ownership of a major refinery in Asia a welcome outlet for this vast supply (Zhdannikov *et al.* 2016).

This short episode of one of the major headline-making state-led acquisitions of recent years exemplifies one of the geopolitical aspects of the Russian competing state. Rosneft profited from the landmark deal, as it made important inroads into Asian markets and expanded its global grip on important refineries for its crude products. From this perspective, the Russian competing state captured an important global asset delivering long-term returns on investment. However, the deal was geopolitically highly sensitive. The security concerns around the Vadinar port are an obvious case in point, but were not the only issue of tension. In the run-up to the negotiations' breakthrough in the autumn of 2016, news sources reported that the planned acquisition almost failed because another party, state-owned Saudi Aramco, also showed interest in Essar Oil (Zhdannikov *et al.* 2016). This reflects the existing geoeconomic competition between Russian and Saudi state-owned firms for high-end refineries in promising global markets, such as has recently also been reported for eastern Europe (Harper 2020). A third geopolitical momentum for the deal was the circumvention of Western sanctions for Rosneft through a financial construct involving Swiss Trafigura and Russian portfolio investor UCP (Pinchuk *et al.* 2016). Identified as the central instrument of Russian geopolitical aggression in Ukraine and with ambitions elsewhere, Rosneft has been on US sanctions lists since 2014, which played a role in the setup of this transaction. All three moments show how the Russian competing state traverses the global competition for economic assets and the geopolitical implications of this competition. Importantly, the Rosneft–Essar deal also shows how the geopolitical dimension of the Russian competing state is not confined to Europe. While many gas and oil conflicts involving geopolitics take place in Russia's closer (Ukraine) or further (western Europe) vicinity,[6] the described advances of Rosneft into Asia expand the grip of the Russian competing state beyond Europe.

This geographical diversification of the Russian competing state became central in early 2022, when the Russian economy started to become crippled through Western sanctions as a consequence of its assault on Ukraine. Whereas the EU and North America were swift to impose financial restrictions on a number of Russian banks, including the central bank, Russian financial and trade ties with other powers remained to some degree intact. Next to many Latin American countries and China, it was especially India that refused to take significant steps to isolate the Russian economy. Part of this strategic consideration is that Russian isolation by the West presents an opportunity for India to increase its imports of cheap Russian crude oil, as it did a few weeks into the war in Ukraine (Menon 2022). Soon thereafter, the Indian authorities began to consider establishing a rupee–rouble mechanism that would directly circumvent a large part of the sanctions against Russian banks and allow, among others, a steady stream of Russian oil to its state-owned Rosneft subsidiaries in India (Verma 2022). The ongoing trade and investment ties of the Russian competing state with powers outside the western hemisphere could help to further stabilize the rouble that at first was in free fall after the initial sanctions package from late February 2022, but recovered afterwards. In addition to central bank measures, it is the existence of these ties and the prospect that they will increasingly replace European export and investment markets that, at least temporarily, provide the last way out for an increasingly isolated Russian economy. Whether the increased imports by India will further strengthen the Russian–Indian relationship remains open at the time of writing. This episode, however, exemplifies another non-EU aspect of the cross-border ties the Russian competing state built, and that could turn out to be a significant factor in circumventing Western sanctions in the future.

Only fuelled by fossil?

Two characteristics of the Russian competing state stand out so far: first, the described turn of strategy and statecraft at the beginning of the 2000s was

---

6. See, for example, Abdelal (2015) for the 2006 and 2009 gas conflicts with Ukraine.

enabled by rising commodity prices, especially oil. This allowed firms like Rosneft to expand further into global markets, capture major assets and become key actors in international politics. Second, the strong ties between the Russian government, oligarchic elites and fossil fuel industry make the Russian competing state especially prone to direct political influence, which is often used to target states (both militarily and geoeconomically) in its European vicinity. Although not every cross-border action undertaken by Russian oil and gas multinationals is of a political nature, the exploitation of these assets by the Russian government to reach geopolitical and geoeconomic goals is evident.

These two elements are, however, only part of the picture of Russian state-led investment in the last two decades. The Russian competing state, especially in its focus on hydrocarbon production, is historically strongly focused on Europe. Beyond ties to its immediate vicinity (e.g. Belarus, Ukraine and Kazakhstan), the Russian competing state is also strongly anchored in Germany, Switzerland, the Netherlands and France. How much of this anchoring in Europe will be left after the war waged on Ukraine in early 2022 and the subsequent sanctions and decoupling attempts by Europe is unclear. However, even beyond Europe, the Russian competing state is active in almost 50 other countries, including India, Turkey and Canada, some of which, like India, do not seem to be willing to break with Russian state-led investment yet. This geographical spread reflects that the Russian competing state not only inherited the hydrocarbon ties to eastern and western Europe from the Cold War, but also branched out into new world regions to capture relevant assets. The non-European investment ties were mostly established during or after the commodity boom of the 2000s, which gave the Russian competing state the opportunity to diversity its portfolio beyond the "old", and now jeopardized, oil and gas ties to Europe.

This initial diversification is also visible in the sectoral composition of the Russian investment profile. Stakes in logistics firm Gefco, uranium mining company Uranium One and several commercial bank subsidiaries illustrate this. The Gefco investment positions the Russian competing state as a major player in the European and international logistics business. Gefco is, among others, one of the major automotive suppliers in Europe and manages an expanding global network of logistic hubs. Through those hubs, Gefco also manages important overall value chains in the metal-working industry and others that will become increasingly important to secure and manage in a geo-economic world (see Chapter 6). Other competing states like France, Germany and some Gulf states are also active in the logistics business, which represents an increasingly central infrastructure in a networked global economy (Coe 2014).

Investment stakes like Gefco show how the Russian competing state is not reducible to its carbon and geopolitical aspects, but uses its commodity revenues to gain a foothold in important nodes and networks of the global political economy. Different from the Chinese case, Russia is not necessarily interested in assets or know-how that would push or complement a certain industrial development strategy. The acquisition of such large logistics firms is rather expected to increase the competitiveness of the Russian economy in general and expand its control of transportation networks into Europe and Asia (Railway Gazette 2012). After all, Russian state capital is both more scarce than Chinese capital and more volatile, because much of Russian state revenue depends on commodity prices. A competing state that has to rely on commodity exports cannot allow for too many trial-and-error investment projects, but needs to be selective in this respect. Consequently, an investment like that in Gefco can also be understood as a "safe bet" that guarantees a steady return on investment from a major global automotive logistics player. An additional factor in this calculation will also be the Western sanctions regime that came into force in 2014 and was significantly expanded in early 2022, and which is unlikely to ever be completely disbanded in relation to Putin's regime. The main question for the non-oil- and gas-related parts of the Russian competing state is whether additional sanctions will specifically target these firms and their financial sources in an attempt to break the rather "soft" geoeconomic tools of the Russian competing state. This also depends on recognizing and evaluating these non-carbon firms as relevant geoeconomic players in the first place. In the case of Gefco, the minority shareholders that are not the Russian state are currently trying to buy back the Russian shares in an attempt to avoid being placed under sanctions (Reuters 2022). Such developments indicate that the dismantling of the Russian competing state might turn out to be one of the main consequences of the sanctions unleashed in early 2022.

A slightly different perspective is offered by non-hydrocarbon investments from Russia that still carry global weight, such as the role of state-owned nuclear company Rosatom. Originating in a Russian state agency, Rosatom became one of the big players in the global nuclear industry. It is engaged in the worldwide managing and constructing of nuclear plants. According to self-disclosure, it owns almost 70 per cent of the global nuclear plant construction market (Rosatom 2018). Notwithstanding the plans of major industrial powers like Germany or South Korea to phase out nuclear power, Rosatom keeps expanding its international network of plants and construction sites. This expansion drive is, however, not without controversy: in many cases, as with planned projects in Turkey, its existing stakes in the Finnish nuclear industry and its plant construction in EU countries like Hungary, Rosatom has already created a (geo)political backlash (Foy 2017). Between 2009 and 2013, Rosatom successively took over Canadian mining company Uranium One, whereby it also gained control of mining licences in the USA. Despite the low amounts of uranium that are being mined in the USA, this deal created a political backlash and was even misused in an attempt by US right-wing media to wrongly accuse former Secretary of State Clinton of "giving away" US national security-relevant uranium supplies to a Russian state-owned company[7].

Cases like Rosatom exemplify why even state-owned firms that on paper look like they are predestined to fulfil geopolitical goals for the Russian state are in fact not reducible to simple foreign policy tools. We need to be careful to distinguish between the clear political employment of state ownership abroad and the political backlash the engagement of state-owned entities creates. The latter is not so much an expression of geopolitical ambition, but rather the backlash created by geoeconomic competition of states as owners in a globalized economy. The aspiration of Rosatom and its owner is not so much to be tools in the hand of the Russian state, but rather to mobilize its vast resources to compete for nuclear leadership in the coming period of fundamental energy transformations.[8] Consequently, even in the light of the harshest sanctions ever imposed on an adversary, in April 2022 the US government and its allies are still wary of adding Rosatom to the sanctions regime against Russia. One of the key reasons are Rosatom's global geoeconomic entanglements that make blacklisting the firm potentially problematic for the energy and nuclear security of a number of states (Nephew 2022). The fact that Rosatom is engaging in geoeconomic competition and is not primarily a geopolitical tool blurs its exact role in Putin's outwards strategy. Naturally, this geoeconomic competition for assets and market share creates (geo)political backlash, but this geopolitical aspect is more a *consequence* of state-led cross-border expansion and not so much its prevailing motive. Hence, even the most "geopolitical" competing state is involved in more geoeconomic forms of global competition, which is further discussed in Chapter 6.

Nord Stream 2 and the (geo)politics of global decarbonization

Cases like Rosatom also show how the fate of the Russian competing state is intertwined with the question of climate change. Much of Rosatom's clout in global geoeconomic competition derives from its ability to tap into a possible void of global energy security between discontinued fossil fuels and globally implementable renewable energy sources coming online. Building on decades

---

7. See Kessler (2017) for a fact check on these claims.
8. See Foy (2017) for a description of these challenges.

of know-how, its strong presence in global markets and its state-led backing, Rosatom is able to compete globally among the top providers of nuclear plants and energy. This diversification of the Russian competing state gives it a possibly important edge in the global climate race to zero carbon emissions, as the initial carve-out from Western sanctions implies.

At the same time, the more "classical" instruments of the Russian competing state are also affected by a changing global energy landscape. For oil firms like Rosneft, the strategic choices are more or less limited: in a world that seeks to rapidly decarbonize, branching out into emerging markets (e.g. through Essar Oil) might be one of the last large-scale attempts to capitalize on a growing global energy need through fossil fuels. For gas providers like Gazprom, the calculation is somewhat different: natural gas can, under optimal circumstances, serve as a transition technology until the maturity and diffusion of renewables is accomplished.[9] The status of gas as (allegedly) comparatively less CO_2 emitting than oil or coal grants firms like Gazprom an advantage in cross-border expansion and even international politics. They are less likely to face immediate existential threats by the growing need to decarbonize, in contrast to firms like Rosneft: the oil giant is already experiencing price conflicts with other non-state-owned oil firms that are being pressured to divest from fossil fuels.[10] The public disputes over the role of gas, oscillating between a "dirty" energy source and a so-called bridge technology, offer firms like Gazprom more strategic possibilities for cross-border engagement.

The large-scale pipeline project Nord Stream 2 is a case in point for this extended strategic repertoire. Many observers, especially from central and eastern Europe (CEE), evaluated the 2015 launch of the Nord Stream 2 construction project as a classical geopolitical move by Russia. The cooperation between Russia and Germany on a second gas pipeline through the Baltic Sea was deemed to serve Russian interests to circumvent Ukraine and other CEE transit countries for Russian gas. This would not only disadvantage these transit countries but also increase the German (and European) dependence on Russian gas. The conflict in eastern Ukraine since 2014 intensified these demands from many CEE and other European countries and urged European leaders to rethink building additional energy ties between the EU and a geopolitically more aggressive Russia (Barteczko *et al.* 2018). Defenders of the project, like large parts of the German political class, often pointed out that Nord Stream 2 would actually be a commercial enterprise, and that rolling back an

---

9. For a comprehensive review see Gürsan and de Gooyert (2021).
10. See Sheppard and Raval (2020) for the dispute between Rosneft and other large oil firms on renewables.

almost finished pipeline of this size would not be economically viable (Knolle & Polityuk 2021). The war waged on Ukraine in early 2022 shattered the illusions about the ability of Germany or other powers to balance its dependence on Russian gas with its political support for CEE countries and especially Ukraine. The *de facto* cancellation of Nord Stream 2 in February 2022 does not do away with the fact that Gazprom and other Russian state-owned fossil fuel firms turned out to indeed be the economic weapon that many feared them to be. In fact, in early 2022 countries like Germany were still importing high volumes of Russian gas because of the lack of alternative sources. The high dependence of European states on Russian gas and oil has also been nurtured over the years by the increasing presence of Russian state-owned (fossil fuel) capital in Europe. The apparent unwillingness of specifically Germany to react to Russia's aggression by cutting off a key funding source for Putin's regime exemplifies this dependence co-created through transnational state capital.

In the long run, these geopolitical questions will be overlain by structural changes in both global energy markets and the decarbonization efforts of recent years. The first point refers to the unprecedented rise of US shale gas production since 2008 (Yergin 2020). While energy scarcity has always been a source of geopolitical tension for the largest industrial power on earth, the discovery and subsequent production of shale gas changed this calculation fundamentally. Instead of being reliant on oil- and gas-exporting countries in the Middle East and elsewhere, in 2016 the USA became an exporter of liquefied natural gas, the transportable form of natural gas. This was not simply an economic boon for the USA, but also had important consequences for the Russian competing state: suddenly, Russian gas was faced with a powerful rival that was keen on taking over export markets in Europe. This meant that European dependency on Russian gas was imperilled, and with it the relative power that companies like Gazprom can project cross-border.[11] Nord Stream 2 can therefore be seen as an attempt to solidify and expand the existing gas ties between western Europe and Russia, and to keep companies like Gazprom competitive in the coming energy transformations. The abrupt halt to this project in 2022 puts a question mark behind the future of this aspect of the Russian competing state.

The second point refers to the fact that while the status of gas as a transition technology is still being debated, the reasonableness of a second major pipeline through the Baltic Sea was much more questionable to begin with. Studies estimated that the role of other gas importers (such as US shale gas),

---

11. For the relation between the US "shale revolution" and Russian gas geopolitics see Yergin (2020).

but especially the projected development of renewables, made Nord Stream 2 *de facto* redundant even before its cancellation.[12] This redundancy of one of the prestige projects of Gazprom, and thus of the Russian competing state, stems from the emerging structural changes through global decarbonization efforts, even beyond any geopolitical calculations. While it is therefore true that gas will be phased out much more slowly than the dirtier coal and oil industries, in the particular case of Nord Stream 2, the Russian competing state will hardly be able to consolidate its position as a major player in the European energy supply, even in a hypothetical post-Putin future. The political support that the project enjoyed, especially in the German political landscape, is gone after the attack on Ukraine, and neither German support nor US hostility towards the project would have altered the structural constraints of a changing energy landscape and the green transition in the long run, which will decide much of the fate of the Russian competing state in the future.

From Russia, with doubts: the future of the Russian competing state

The expansion of Russian state capital into the transnational agency space of the global economy has in many ways been both vigorous and unfulfilled at the same time. The reconcentration of power and state capital in the hands of the Putin regime and the commodity supercycle of the 2000s, enabling the growth of fossil fuel firms, paved the way for a considerable growth of Russian cross-border engagement. Large-scale takeovers like the Essar Oil case, or the expansion of Gazprom and Rosatom to become some of the most relevant actors in global energy matters, speak for themselves. They exemplify how Russian state capital has been employed to seek dominance in global industries (Rosatom), or to remake European energy infrastructures (Gazprom). At the same time, these developments were mitigated by the *de facto* end of the commodity boom in the mid-2010s and increasing geopolitical confrontation with Europe and the USA. Different from other cases, the "smooth" growth of the Russian competing state was inhibited by the drop in oil and gas revenues, on which not only the Putin regime but also its state-owned multinationals depend. Other commodity-exporting competing states, such as the Gulf states and Norway, funnel state-owned capital into SWFs, which are more flexible instruments than SOEs. They can consequently diversify more easily and thus absorb falling commodity prices to a certain degree. The concentration of Russian state capital in large gas and oil firms furthermore increases the risk

---

12. See the study by Neumann *et al.* (2018), which is an important reference point in the German debate.

of being targeted by economic sanctions, especially if they are employed in geopolitical conflicts. Long-term sanction targets like Rosneft have again been constrained both at the managerial as well as the operational and financial level by Western sanctions in the current war on Ukraine. Hence, the power of the Russian competing state with its capital concentrated in a few select firms also creates little wiggle room, and exposes itself to both commodity price volatilities and tightening sanction regimes. At the moment of writing, it is hard to imagine a viable future for the carbon-fuelled Russian competing state, especially in a more geoeconomic and protectionist world.

Subject to a political rehabilitation of Russian foreign investment in a post-Putin future, the destiny of the Russian competing state would also depend on other industries and actors than its hydrocarbon giants. One possible avenue discussed in this chapter is nuclear energy, for which Rosatom is the main proponent. Despite the abandoning of nuclear power by some major industrial nations, global decarbonization efforts might in some world regions be easier to achieve through nuclear than through "semi-dirty" technologies like gas. Depending on how global energy consumption develops in scale and diversity, nuclear is considered a serious option, especially for emerging economies.[13] Rosatom is already tapping into this possible opportunity through cross-border investment, but also faces some resistance from actors evaluating it as a geopolitical tool in the hands of the Russian state. Another less likely possibility for Russian state capital expansion is finance. Russian state-owned banks have been investing cross-border for some time, into Turkey (Sberbank), Austria, Germany, France (VTB Group) and the Netherlands (Alfa Bank) among others (see also Atnashev & Vashakmadze 2016). During the 2000s, bank internationalization was considered a promising avenue for Russian state capital to go beyond its strong presence in CEE. However, Russian state-connected financial firms have also suffered sanctions-related setbacks: for example, Sberbank had to sell its largest foreign stake in well-performing Denizbank in 2019, also partly because of sanction effects. This move is also part of a broader strategy of a refocusing on the Russian home market instead of further international expansion[14].

In sum, the rise of the Russian competing state after the end of the commodity boom remains to some degree unfulfilled, and its future more than uncertain. One major contributing factor to this diagnosis is the tactical rather than strategic nature of the Russian competing state. This implies that the high degree of control over assets and investment is indeed employed cross-border, but not explicitly with a visible long-term vision. Whereas other players like

---

13. In a 2019 report, the International Energy Agency advocates for using nuclear to reach ambitious climate goals, see IEA (2019).

14. See the respective quote on a strategy change by the Sberbank CEO in Daily Sabah (2019).

China – or those states with financial strategies discussed in the next chapter – exhibit a mid- to long-term strategic oversight over the goals and means of state capital transnationalization, the Russian approach is rather reactive and ad hoc. This has, for example, been visible in the "gas wars" with Ukraine in 2006 and 2009, as well as in the sanctions-forced retreat from its Denizbank involvement in 2019. In cases where strategic projects are discernible, as in the Nord Stream 2 case, backlashes caused by Russian (geo)political aggression inhibit their successful realization. On top of this, the climate question is lurking in the background of the future development of the Russian competing state. Recent analyses suggest that the awareness of the impact of the energy transition on fossil fuel-exporting economies is low among Russian elites: whereas states like Saudi Arabia display concern and strategic planning for a post-carbon age, Russian policy-makers decidedly bet on a future of hydrocarbon *scarcity* (Bradshaw *et al.* 2019). The outcome of this bet will not only shape much of the fate of the Russian competing state, but also of the Russian population in the decades to come. The Western condemnation of Putin's attack on Ukraine is further decreasing the scope that Russian transnational state capital has, which is now entirely reliant on its economic partners outside Europe and North America. Although India and China, as two of the largest global economic powers, have signalled that they intend to take a neutral stance towards Russia's aggression in Ukraine, the chances of the Russian competing state to play any relevant role after the war in Ukraine are dwindling by the day.

France and Germany: statism gone European

The last case study of controlling strategies is Germany and France. I discuss them together, because they share a similar transnationalization strategy that builds on a legacy of national champions. As discussed in Chapter 2, those national champions were built and nurtured during the postwar years of intensified build-up of industrial policy capacities. Generally speaking, national champions are not necessarily state-owned firms: the politics of choosing, possibly merging, financially supporting and protecting firms does not need to involve an actual ownership stake by the state. However, given the historical emergence of national champions in industries prone to state ownership, such as energy or defence, many firms are actually state-owned. This is, for example, the case for EDF (France) and Deutsche Bahn (DB) (Germany). In some cases, states retained a "golden share" that was often tied to a veto power such as in Engie (France) or Telekom (Germany).

(Internationalizing) national champions are then the basis of both the French and the German competing states. Both differ, however, in how their respective champions emerged historically. In the mid-twentieth century, France was next to Britain as the role model for an activist industrial policy that gave birth to large conglomerates and utility firms. The productivity catch-up of European and Japanese firms with their US competitors in the postwar period,[15] as well as fears of an emerging "technology gap" between the USA and Europe (Owen 2012: 5), led French politicians to engage in serious capacity building in the 1960s and 1970s. In addition to encouraging private mergers, and acting as a "dirigiste" state in industrial planning, state ownership was a major strategic aspect at the time (Owen 2012: 12). Precursors of today's large (inter)national champions like Airbus or Engie were created through these policies.

By the 1980s, France had a strong portfolio of national champions, many of them state-owned and in key sectors such as energy or industrial engineering. The rising privatization pressures within neoliberal globalization in the early 1990s, as well as the European single-market formation process, forced the French state to undermine parts of this basis. At the time, French industrial policy largely gave up on what Elie Cohen dubbed "High-Tech Colbertism", with a strong sectoral focus on "grand projects" and national champions (Cohen: 2007), and adapted to the horizontal industrial policy approach promoted by the European single-market framework. Large-scale targeted sectoral mobilization was no longer an option under the new European competitiveness regime.

At the same time, the French state retained strong institutions that adapted to these changing global conditions. In the energy sector, for example, the former Direction générale de l'énergie et des matières premières agency supervised and during the 1990s also transformed former national champions into international champions (Viallet-Thévenin 2015). Other more broadly conceptualized SOE management agencies like the Agence des Participations de l'État (APE) were founded in the early 2000s, at a similar time to China's SASAC. APE embodies the French "shareholding state", by managing several dozen state stakes in privatized companies. The creation of agencies like APE has been interpreted as the financialization of state–SOE relations in France, which moves away from the dirigiste vision of the twentieth century (Coutant 2014). At the same time, recent strategic updates of the APE indicate a "revised doctrine" towards a more targeted investment strategy that prioritizes strategic and public service companies (APE 2017). Almost all of the managed French SOEs are today internationalized, mostly European, heavyweights such as Renault, Engie or EDF.

---

15. For a calculation of productivity growth in different world regions and time periods see Maddison (1987: 650).

The German case differs historically from the French as state ownership played much less of a role in the development path after the Second World War. Different from a dirigiste approach, the German "social market economy" (*Soziale Marktwirtschaft*) essentially combined ordoliberal economic policies with a strong export orientation. Andrew Shonfield aptly described the German postwar model as "organized private enterprise" (Shonfield 1969: 239), which displayed a postwar scepticism towards a strong state role in economic activity itself. In fact, overall state ownership decreased constantly in the aftermath of the Second World War (Fohlin 2005: 233). At the same time, Germany's utility firms were, like in many other developed countries, in state hands for the most part of the twentieth century. During the privatization waves of the 1980s and 1990s, some of those utilities were (partly) privatized (Vogelsang 1988). While many remain in full state ownership today, others like the former Telekom (today globally known as T Mobile) or car manufacturer Volkswagen retained a "golden share" for the (local) government.

In the mid-1990s, the privatization debates also reached the largest and most subsidized SOE, the railway operator DB. The transformation into a quasi-private enterprise in 1994 was a controversial move, as was the planned but never fulfilled public listing of the firm. At the same time, the restructuring of the old DB state agency into a holding company consisting of several subsidiaries opened the possibility to compete on international markets. A similar development emerged with the partly privatized Telekom, which has now expanded into Europe and the USA, among others. Internationalizing from a large domestic market, and with the help of decade-long heavy subsidization by the German government, firms like DB and its different subsidiaries quickly captured large market segments, especially within Europe. A key sector of this internationalization effort is transportation and logistics, which gained increasing relevance from the 2000s onwards, as logistics and delivery networks became increasingly crucial for global economic competition (Coe 2014).

These different historical circumstances led the present German competing state to be significantly smaller than the French in terms of transnational SOEs and also with regards to total state-led investment. At the same time, the fewer German SOEs managed to enter and compete within major European markets, and they represent some of the most valuable European firms today. This bundling of economic power in a handful of strong players makes the German competing state a relevant global economic player.

Europe as a playground

Interestingly enough, the targets of German and French internationalization efforts are located mostly in Europe. Different from the more globalized

Chinese, Norwegian or Gulf investments, France and even more so Germany are mostly "transnationalizing" state investment in their immediate vicinity: over 90 per cent of French and over 92 per cent of German state investment is located in other European states. The fact that Europe itself is a key target for the lion's share of transnational state investment in general partly explains this focus (see Chapter 3). The historical emergence of asset and know-how concentration in national champions, in combination with the creation of the European single market, granted those firms a privileged position for capturing European market shares. This pattern of Europe as a "playground" for state-owned multinationals should, however, not obscure the fact that their European standing forms a strong basis for worldwide internationalization: state-owned firms like GeoPost or Transdev control wide-ranging global networks of, for example, logistics and transportation. The European focus of French and German state-led investment is hence the first dimension of a broader internationalization strategy.

The French investments are spearheaded by state-owned energy giant EDF. The company has a strong presence in the UK, where it participates in several large-scale nuclear projects. Lately, it also increased its presence in renewables, making it one of the key players in the UK's race to net zero. Since its entrance into the British market in 2002, EDF has established itself as a major energy provider for the country through targeted acquisitions and project participation. EDF also branched out into other European economies, for instance by acquiring Italian gas and electricity provider Edison in 2012. The strategic nature of taking over a globally active energy provider became palpable when EDF, despite previous countervailing statements, delisted Edison after taking over close to 100 per cent of its shares (Reuters 2012).

EDF itself is managed within the APE framework, which also contains other (inter)national champions like Airbus. Another significant majority-owned international player from the APE portfolio is La Poste. The former state monopoly developed into a major logistics and delivery company in Europe and beyond through its cross-border subsidiary GeoPost. As one of the fastest-growing European logistics firms, GeoPost owns a portfolio of European delivery companies such as the DPD Group. After energy provision and logistics, transportation is a third major sector where French cross-border ownership is present. Through transportation firms like Transdev, which is globally active, the French state retains a firm grip on the respective markets in countries like Germany, Australia and the Netherlands. A relevant competing ground for firms like Transdev is especially the UK transportation market, where French, Dutch and German state-owned firms compete in the UK railway market.

The German strategy is even more focused at the European level, with its top-ten investment targets being other European states. Similar to France, logistics and transportation play a paramount role for the German strategy. This is first and foremost the case for the DB subsidiary Schenker, which managed to become one of the largest logistics and supply chain managers in Europe. With subsidiaries distributed around the world, Schenker forms a global logistics network similar to GeoPost (discussed above). Profiting from the domestic market position and know-how of DB, the success of these internationalization efforts is built on the basis of a formerly national champion. Similar to Schenker, the railway logistics firm DB Cargo (another subsidiary of DB) is invested in various European states such as Poland, the UK and France. Even more concentrated on one specific national champion than in the French case, the German competing state successfully established itself as one of the major forces of controlling global logistics and supply chain networks.

Different from the French case, however, energy and other utilities do not play a significant role for the rest of German foreign state-led investment. Most of the German state-owned utility firms remain focused on the domestic market. Instead, DB leads the way through its railway-operating subsidiaries like Arriva. Branched out in various European countries, Arriva has been one of the main operators in the UK railway market, where it competed with other European state-owned operators. This engagement of German (and other) state-owned firms in the "privatized" British market has led to critical debates on the role of foreign powers controlling the UK's national infrastructure. In early 2020, Arriva even lost its franchise for operating railways in northern England after the quality of services declined over the years (Zasiadko 2020). Instead, the UK government renationalized this part of railway operations in order to prop up the ailing infrastructure. These sobering experiences for DB and its subsidiaries indicate that competing for passenger transportation markets might not be the future of the German competing state. Rather, the paramount role logistics play in a globalized economy seems to be the strategic focus of the German competing state, for which its DB subsidiaries provide a strong backbone.

A major difference between the German and French competing states is the lower degree of centralization of state-owned assets and their management in Germany. Whereas French agencies like APE provide a strategic platform for bundling and directing state-owned resources, Germany does not have such a functional unit. At the same time, calls for sovereign instruments that would increase the agency of the German competing state are getting louder. In the latest iteration, a discussion around the creation of a German SWF emerged after the government barely managed to fend off an unwanted

Chinese takeover of the German electricity grid firm 50Hertz in 2018. Previous discussions about a German SWF included motives like recycling its export surplus or stabilizing the eurozone. In any case, introducing a state fund of any sort would upgrade the German competing state in a similar way to a state asset management agency, and extend its agency options significantly.

Merging powers? European champions in the making

Such an upgrade of European competing states is also currently being dis-cussed at the European level itself. In 2019, a Franco-German strategic paper outlined the contours of what both governments consider a "genuine European industrial policy" (BMBF 2019: 1) for the coming decade. Such a strategic pro-ject is supposed to work only through a common approach, in which European countries bundle their powers to compete on global markets. One of the main motivations for the call was the failed merger between German and French railway champions Siemens and Alstom, which was blocked by the European Commission on competition grounds. The 2019 strategy paper consequently calls for "much more strategic thinking than in the past" (*ibid.*), where the competitiveness principles overrode the strategic interest of creating European champions. While France and Germany were leading the initiative, they were soon flanked by other major European economies in demanding laxer rules for European mergers and other forms of state aid (Braun *et al.* 2020). These attempts aim to redefine what competitiveness means in a geostrategic envi-ronment, where state-backed actors like China operate under a different set of strategic premises than the "old" European level-playing-field approach.

National champions and the mobilization of state-owned and state-directed capital thereby plays a paramount role in this new industrial strategy. Besides protectionist moves and (in)direct state financing of competitive sectors and firms, actively building and developing European champions in key sectors is at the heart of this new strategic outlook. One policy instrument that has been advocated in this direction are the "Important Projects of Common European Interest" (IPICEI) since 2018. They promote and finance European coopera-tion between respective (niche) champions in order to develop strategically important industries such as semiconductors or hydrogen fuels. Going beyond a focus on state-owned firms, the basic idea of IPICEI is to bring together "national" champions through state funding to cooperate on solutions with which they then can compete outside of Europe for the global market shares of the future. Such an approach represents a pragmatic attempt to bring the new European industrial strategy to life. In the coming decade, these strate-gic impulses are expected to increase with the "double challenge" of climate change and new geoeconomic rivalries on the horizon of European politics.

Although doubts about the viability and long-term prospects of these strategic changes remain, they represent a step towards a possible European competing state. Existing critical political economy research on European state formation has stressed that these processes are contested, fragmented and rarely straightforward (van Apeldoorn & Horn 2018). The interesting question from the perspective developed in this book is which role state capital can and will play in these developments. Two points can be made here. First, the financing and development of European champions is at the heart of the new European industrial strategy. Without companies that are able to bundle know-how, assets and political power, a confrontation with Chinese and other competitors on global markets is futile. In this respect, state capital will play a key role in supporting these developments within and beyond the EU. Given the differences in the ability to mobilize state capital in various sectors (think about the differences between France and Germany alone), different "national" competing states are likely to yield more power at the European level. This creates the potential for new power struggles within the EU along different political economy axes than in the last decades.

Second, the concrete formation and shape of a possible EU-level competing state will crucially be driven through the interaction with other great powers, most notably China. In 2022 the EU is contemplating issues like a "geopolitical Commission", "digital sovereignty" or "strategic autonomy" through the prism of systemic and geoeconomic competition with China and partly the USA. As scholars of state capitalism have argued, the rise of a statist China in the global political economy induces similar but uneven responses across the board of capitalist forms (Alami *et al.* 2022). Such responses are not necessarily emulations; hence, the EU will not suddenly renationalize its internationally competitive firms and install an authoritarian political system to meet the "China challenge". Rather, the EU and its member states are likely to build on existing path dependencies and reintroduce well-known forms of industry coordination and competition to the political agenda. The described revival of Franco-German industrial policies is a case in point: it builds on a historical legacy of industrial strategy and national (state-owned) champions, which is updated to accommodate new geoeconomic rivalries in the twenty-first century.

The future of European competing states

The China challenge also points us to the possible futures of European competing states. Two aspects are crucial in this respect: the "active" and "passive" characteristics of competing states. For the first point, states like France and Germany can build on their existing transnational state investment ties to further exploit the transnational agency space through state-owned means.

Far from running into issues, as we saw in the Russian example, both are well positioned in important global industries which will only increase in their relevance for the global economy. Their involvement in logistics and transportation networks through state-led investment, in particular, grants both states privileged and powerful positions to start with. Recent scholarship has argued that infrastructure-led development will play an increasingly important role, especially in its transnational forms (Schindler & Kanai 2021). Such a new global development regime crucially involves logistical questions related to the realization of large-scale infrastructure projects. The position of European states like France or Germany in these and related industries is an important building block for the future of European competing states (or that of a united Europe) in the face of new global geopolitical realities.

On the "passive" side, many EU states as well as the EU itself for the first time introduced comprehensive investment screening mechanisms that especially target various forms of state-led or state-backed investment. In 2020, a European coordination mechanism came into effect, which is supposed to facilitate and standardize investment screening among EU member states (De Jong & Zwartkruis 2020). States like Germany and France adopted wide-ranging measures and engaged in the curbing and blocking of especially Chinese state-led investment (Stompfe 2020). Such efforts to hamper foreign state-led investment can be regarded as the other side of competing state policies. They take aim at curbing the investment activities of other competing states in their jurisdiction, which is – at least in the political discussions – often associated with technology or know-how transfer (Babic & Dixon 2022).

The EU and European member states thereby follow a path that emerges out of an older policy paradigm: for a long time Europe championed a global level-playing-field approach vis-à-vis other global economic powers (see van Miert 1998). Since the intensification of global rivalries in the last years, and the subsequently mentioned "geopoliticization" (Meunier & Nicolaidis 2019) of European foreign economic policies, the EU opted to foreclose some of these earlier commitments to an open global economy. How far this will spill over to other policy fields remains open. However, it shows that the repertoire of European competing states goes beyond "active" instruments. The two main players in this constellation – Germany and France – are expected to push for further strategic reorientation in an increasingly geoeconomic environment. The future of these European competing states hence depends on the willingness to further transform domestically, as well as on China's development trajectory, which is closely intertwined with the fate of the US and European political economies.

5

Strategies of the competing state: financial strategies

After discussing controlling strategies in the previous chapter, this one deals with what I described in Chapter 3 as the financial strategies of states as global owners. Financial strategies can take different forms, but their most characteristic aspect is that a majority of a state's cross-border investment is located in portfolio investment.[1] Such an amount of ownership held is, *ceteris paribus*, unlikely to end up in significant corporate control. The goal of the owning state is hence not to exert a high degree of control, or to engage in asset capture through cross-border investment. Rather, financial strategies indicate an interest in returns on investment – that is, financial profit – as the overarching motive of such investment. The two cases addressed in this chapter – Norway and Singapore – each engage in different forms of financial strategies. While Norway employs an almost "pure" financial strategy, Singapore's profile is more mixed and complex. Furthermore, and similar to the discussed controlling strategies, the goals, abilities and consequences of these strategies differ markedly once we zoom in on those cases.

Norway: turning diseases into assets

In terms of GDP per capita, Norway is among the richest countries in the world. At the same time, it has an unusually high state involvement in its economy: the Norwegian state is invested in over a third of the Oslo stock

---

1. Portfolio investment includes equity stakes that amount to less than 10 per cent of a company's shares. See also UNCTAD (2011: 28), which argues that effective corporate control starts at around 10 per cent of shares held.

exchange (Lie 2016), has an off-the-charts relation between equity owner-ship and GDP (Kim 2021) and controls the largest SWF in history. How did a state with a relatively modest tax base of slightly over five million inhabitants become such a powerful force in global capitalism? Two cornerstones are important for the evolution of the Norwegian competing state. The first is the postwar rise of the state as investor and owner. As a late industrializer, the Norwegian economy lacked a robust investment base, which was partly rem-edied by increased state investment in these years (Lie 2016: 911). Similar to other European states in the postwar years, Norway developed a corporatist and centralist governance model, including (limited) state ownership in key sectors (Christensen 2005: 724; see also Lie 2016). Second, this emerging state ownership model encountered an oil boom in the 1970s. Towards the end of the 1960s, the discovery of North Sea oil fields within Norwegian jurisdic-tion initiated an exploration boom. To keep control of the newly emerging revenue stream, state-owned Statoil was created in 1972. Through a close and controlled state management via Statoil over the next decades, the state own-ership and production of the oil stemming from the Norwegian Continental Shelf even increased over time (Thurber & Istad 2011: 14). This strong role of state ownership did not significantly decrease during the privatization waves of the 1990s, where Statoil was only partially listed. In fact, the large-scale merger with the fossil fuel division of state-owned Norsk Hydro in 2007 is a clear competing state move set to create a "unified Norwegian champion with the cash flow and scale to compete more effectively abroad" (Thurber & Istad 2011: 17).

These two basic elements – an active (ownership) role of the state and state-controlled oil revenues – laid the foundation for the rise of the Norwegian SWF as a global financial heavyweight. In order to avoid the economic risks associated with high commodity exports – from the oil crises of the 1970s to the so-called "Dutch disease" (Corden 1984) – the Norwegian government established an oil-funded SWF in 1990. The Government Pension Fund Global (GPF-G) basically recycles oil revenues in global financial markets, and does so successfully: in 2019 alone, it documented a return of 20 per cent of its invest-ments and was invested in over 9,000 companies worldwide. This amounts to around 1.5 per cent of all global stocks and a value of over $1 trillion in AuM (CNBC 2020). A steady flow of oil revenues, in combination with a strong state grip on both their realization and reinvestment, have resulted in the Norwegian competing state occupying an extraordinary position within global financial markets. By owning a significant portion of those markets, the Norwegian SWF is able to move them with its (dis)investment decisions. This became palpable in 2019, when its announcement to sell its stakes from oil-producing firms made the fund a front-runner in global financial decarbonization efforts

(Arvin 2021b). The Norwegian decision is anticipated to influence and pressure other large equity funds like Blackrock or Vanguard, with whom it shares important features such as their sheer size, investment strategies and relevance for sustainability goals[2].

The integration of a rather state-centred and "closed" Norwegian economy into global production and investment circuits was hence made possible through both the strong grip of the state on oil production and its revenues and the fact that these revenues could be reinvested via global financial markets. This recycling led to a partial decoupling of oil sales and (future) state revenues. In turn, the weight and power of the Norwegian competing state increased over time and turned a rather "small" economy into one of the major global financial players. Next to securing the welfare of current and future Norwegian society, the rise within the transnational agency space granted the Norwegian competing state a major power position within international finance, with a very different strategic outlook than other competing states.

Liquidity as strategy

The strategies surveyed in this book so far aim at controlling their invested firms. Financial strategies are at first sight less intuitive: states that own large amounts of corporate equity could also choose to acquire and control whole firms, instead of dispersing their investment across many different non-controlling portfolio stakes. This is even more the case for the Norwegian example, as the sheer size of its AuM makes it one of the largest states as owners globally. Two reasons stand out as possible motivations for financial strategies. First, the goal of the competing state is not to capture assets, technologies or other relevant equity "stored" in large firms outside one's borders, but rather a steady return on investment. This means that controlling a firm does not necessarily lead to higher returns on investment, which is in most cases also not the goal of controlling strategies. Second, if profit is the underlying motivation for state capital transnationalization, diversification through portfolio investment increases the likelihood of a higher return on investment and minimizes the risk of losses. By not "betting" on a handful of large SOEs and their chances at realizing a steady profit, financial strategies hedge themselves against volatility, especially in commodity markets where many SOEs are directly or indirectly involved. Hence, financial strategies allow competing states like Norway to reap the financial benefits of a globalized economy, without appearing as

---

2. See Fichtner and Heemskerk (2020) for a discussion of the asset managers running these large funds.

predatory "state capitalists" that supposedly threaten the liberal order and free market capitalism[3].

One key consequence of this strategic profile is that it equips the Norwegian competing state with large pools of mostly liquid capital. Almost three-quarters of the total GPF-G investment is located in equities, and the rest (one-quarter) is almost entirely in fixed income, with only about 2 to 3 per cent being invested in real estate. In total, over 90 per cent of total Norwegian transnational state capital is invested in portfolio stakes. As a consequence, both the financial and political flexibility of the Norwegian competing state is comparatively high: diversification and disinvestment because of financial losses or political untenability are easier when the invested state capital is liquid and not stored in large, majority-owned corporations and similar assets. The Norwegian competing state itself is a prime example of this distinction: it was considerably easier for the mostly portfolio-invested Norwegian SWF to withdraw its fossil fuel state investment by 2021 than to "truly" decarbonize by cutting its reliance on oil production revenues (Arvin 2021b). The latter investment is mostly stored in majority-owned firms like Statoil, which can be regarded as illiquid state capital.

Citizen of everywhere

For its outwards investment, the Norwegian competing state relies overwhelmingly on portfolio investment. This liquidity also leads to a massive geographical spread. The Norwegian state is invested in 85 countries around the world, which makes it the geographically most comprehensive state as owner. It is invested in all world regions, and holds significant ownership stakes in the American stock market as well as in German car makers and Japanese multinationals. The same diversity applies to its invested sectors, which range from manufacturing to energy generation, to real estate construction and financial firms. The exploitation of the transnational agency space by the Norwegian competing state is truly global, spanning both the Global South and North, and a variety of industries and firms. Different from other states that employ controlling strategies in their immediate vicinity, the relative liquidity of Norwegian state capital makes it a citizen of everywhere.

Despite this broad profile, there is a clear concentration of Norwegian state capital within the transatlantic sphere, especially within US stock markets (Table 5.1). More than 40 per cent of its total investment is located in the

---

3. Such as is argued by Bremmer (2010) for states like China or Russia and their investment vehicles.

Table 5.1 Top-five targets of Norwegian foreign state investment

Target	Percentage of total investment
USA	41.4
Japan	9.8
Germany	9.4
UK	7.7
Canada	3.5

USA, while around 10 per cent are each invested in Germany and Japan. Other relevant targets are the UK, China, South Korea, Canada and Australia, but each is significantly lower than the US investment. Such a focus on the largest and most attractive equity market in the world is not an anomaly: the transnational agency space is an *open* but not a *flat* space. This means that investment will always be unequally distributed. The unevenness of the global political economy is also reflected in these capital flows, which aim to generate a viable and stable profit for the Norwegian state. Directing portfolio investment to US and European markets is likely to guarantee those aims, as the financial track record of the Norwegian SWF and other vehicles of the last years exemplifies.

Being such a large and diversified owner, the Norwegian competing state creates surprisingly little backlash from the host states of its investments. This has also to do with the fact that the vast majority of Norwegian state capital is portfolio investment, which is a (geo)politically rather non-suspicious investment form. Beyond this, however, it is especially the investment philosophy of the Norwegian SWF that shapes the image of a "good" institutional investor. Early on, the fund adopted an "ethical mandate" (Clark & Monk 2010b), which allows it to distinguish between "good" and "bad" investments in socio-economic and sustainability terms. This mandate largely derives from the involvement of the Norwegian parliament and finance ministry in developing the concrete investment mandate for the fund. Hence, the domestic legitimacy basis of the Norwegian competing state is fairly broad, which also influences its international reputation when large volumes of state capital are invested outside Norway's borders.

Moving markets, navigating climate change

This solid legitimacy of the Norwegian competing state often puts it centre stage in discussions on climate change mitigation. Early on, many voices from in and outside Norway demanded a stricter orientation towards practices of decarbonization and green investment. These demands were also possible on the basis of the strong transparency policy of the GPF-G, which allowed the public to monitor its sustainability pledges and shortcomings. In addition, the sheer size of the Norwegian competing state – which is one of the two largest states as corporate owners globally – increases the weight of its (dis)investment decisions for global decarbonization efforts. By owning a significant share of global equity markets, the decisions of the Norwegian SWF can and do influence and move global markets.

Disinvestment from fossil fuels via portfolio investment is at the same time only one side of the issue. Lately, the Norwegian state has been criticized for, on the one hand, pioneering carbon disinvestment efforts, and on the other hand, still being crucially reliant on fossil fuel revenues to fund its investment activities. What is more, state investment is also used for funding fossil fuel activities, despite pledges for rapid decarbonization.[4] A 2021 report on the possibilities of a state-led green industrial policy in Norway carves out these issues precisely and suggests ways forward (Kattel *et al.* 2021). Accordingly, one major leverage that Norway has are some of the elementary tools of its competing state, such as its ownership stakes in fossil fuel industries as well as a high-volume investment vehicle that can be reorganized to finance a sustainability transition.[5] While these potentials are enormous with regards to the endowments of the Norwegian competing state, clear-eyed political will and mobilization will be required in the coming decade.

The emerging picture of the Norwegian competing state is hence complex. On the one hand, its size and corresponding power in global markets in combination with its ethical investment mandate and pledges for decarbonization represent a role model for other institutional investors like pension funds and asset managers that are also able to move markets with their investment strategies. On the other hand, a historical legacy of relying strongly on oil revenues, which still plays a crucial role in the politico-economic configuration of the Norwegian competing state, complicates a straightforward path to effective decarbonization. It is clear, however, that the build-up of massive assets and a highly successful cross-border investment strategy by the Norwegian competing state allows Norway to be in a position to politically and economically influence its further development strategy in a changing global order.

---

4. See Kattel *et al.* (2021: 9) for a discussion of various fossil-fuel projects funded by GPF-G capital.
5. Kattel and colleagues, for example, argue that "[r]eorienting investment strategies of sovereign wealth funds towards the green sector would bring some USD 8.2 trillion into climate action finance" (Kattel *et al.* 2021: 27).

Small state in global markets

As we have seen, the Norwegian case is one of the major examples of the competing state form. Its take-off in the 1990s occurred precisely during the heyday of neoliberal globalization, and its strategy is clearly aimed at reaping the benefits of global markets: vehicles like GPF-G invest exclusively outside of Norway's borders. Backed by massive oil revenues, a highly qualified asset management workforce from the Norwegian central bank and the historical experience of other nations when it comes to the mismanagement of commodity booms, it exploited the investment opportunities arising within the transnational agency space. This illustrates very well how financial globalization from the 1990s onwards was the major enabling factor for the Norwegian competing state to thrive on its oil reserves, instead of being fully dependent on them. State power was fused and leveraged through state-led participation in global financial markets, although through different strategies than in cases like China or elsewhere.

Norway therefore represents a curious case of what Peter Katzenstein once called "small states in world markets" (Katzenstein 1985). Katzenstein explained how "small" European states successfully navigate global economic change by combining economic openness with domestic corporatist structures. These corporatist structures accordingly compensate domestic groups which would otherwise be disadvantaged by economic openness, for example when it comes to price volatilities for certain products or increased competitive pressure reducing employment in certain sectors. This dealing with a world of embedded liberalism – that is, mostly of free trade with limited cross-border financial flows – however, demanded adjustment in the 1990s with the advent of neoliberal globalization. Many of these small states adapted to now *global* markets, for example by becoming global financial centres (the Netherlands) or by cumbersome industrial restructuring (Sweden).

Norway, however, pursued a relatively unique path by actively exploiting globalized markets, especially financial ones. Instead of adapting mainly domestically, Norway proactively pursued external adaptation, inserting itself as a *state* in global financial markets. The recycling of oil revenues into its SWF and the subsequent exploitation of global investment opportunities was from the Norwegian perspective an extremely successful adaptation strategy to neoliberal globalization. The birth and the rise of the Norwegian competing state created large-scale opportunities and hence also financial wiggle room for a small state in global markets. While the build-up of a muscular Norwegian competing state is but only one aspect of its broader development model, it is a crucial one: as a small country in global markets, it became one of the largest global asset owners, and a powerful force within global capitalism.

Different from Katzenstein's analysis in the 1980s, Norway did not adapt by *internal* restructuring alone, but also by proactively utilizing the *external* possibilities of the emerging transnational agency space.

This relatively unique position of the Norwegian competing state is today once again being challenged by new and fundamental economic and political changes. The convenient revenue stream from fossil fuel extraction will come under severe pressure in the next decade, and other institutional investors like the "Big Three" passive asset managers are on the way to dominating whole stock exchanges through their business model.[6] On top of this, a more hostile and geoeconomic global environment might be less conducive for investment strategies like the Norwegian one. As a "citizen of everywhere", the Norwegian SWF has so far avoided clashes with the host states of its investments. This could, however, become difficult in times when financial power slowly shifts towards Asia, and especially China, whose financial markets also become attractive investment targets for institutional investors. Regulatory and political backlashes are a real possibility in a multipolar world economy. The Norwegian competing state hence stands yet again before another fundamental transformation in a post-neoliberal global order, just as it did 30 years ago.

Singapore: liberal statism in a changing global order

The last illustration of a competing state is Singapore, which is both similar and fundamentally different from the Norwegian example. In terms of similarity, Singapore is also a small state in a global economy that employs state-owned vehicles – like its two SWFs – to reap the benefits of a globalized economy. At the same time, however, Singapore is an extremely open economy and a *de facto* offshore financial centre, attracting large volumes of foreign capital (Garcia-Bernardo *et al.* 2017). This differentiates it from other states as owners with SWFs like many Gulf states, which are extremely closed economies. The Singaporean political economy hence combines the "statist" aspect of large state ownership with the more "neoliberal" aspect of being an a largely open economy. This also has consequences for its standing as a competing state: it is one of the few countries worldwide to attract comparative amounts of state investment as it sends cross-border, and as such is one of a handful of so-called sender-targets (see Babic *et al.* 2020). Singapore does so at a high level that is comparable to other large-scale owners and targets like France or the USA. For these reasons, Singapore presents an interesting case of a mixed financial

---

6. See Fichtner and Heemskerk (2020) for an in-depth study of the financial eco-system and resulting power of the "Big Three".

profile, which combines the pursuit of returns on investment with a strategic edge that grants the government some control over its invested firms.

This strategy of what I call *liberal statism* stems from Singapore's historical legacy as a small state in East Asia. Different from Norway and other competing states, Singapore could not rely on vast oil or other commodity reserves in the mid-twentieth century to fund its competing state. After its independence from the state union with Malaysia in 1965, the government instead pursued a development model that has been dubbed a "rational *dirigisme*" (Huff 1995: 736, emphasis in original). This model involved a high degree of state planning, similar to other fast-developing Asian countries like South Korea. At the same time, the long-time People's Action Party government opened up Singapore for foreign investment in order to counter the country's lack of productive investment in manufacturing and other relevant industries (Siddiqui 2010: 4). The quick build-up of industrial capacities made Singapore a manufacturing exporter, with the share of the manufacturing industry almost doubling for both total employment and GDP between 1960 and the early 1990s (Huff 1995: 739). In an era when productivity growth was slowing across the industrialized world, Singapore achieved constantly high growth rates and established itself as a high-income and open, but at the same time state-led, economy.

An early manifestation of this described "rational *dirigisme*" is the Economic Development Board (EDB), founded in the beginning of the 1960s. The EDB's mission statement reflects the liberal statist nature of the Singaporean economic model by describing its task as a government agency as "investment promotion and industry development" (EDB 2021: 2). Through reaching out and building global networks of investors and joint ventures with domestic firms, the EDB built a solid foundation for the Singaporean competing state that emerged later on. It helped to establish Singapore as a global hub for foreign investment, while at the same time functioning as investor in, and developer of, domestic industries (Pek 2017). The fact that the EDB has coordinated industrial and development strategy in Singapore for 60 years illustrates the strong anchoring of competing state policies in the political-economic history of the country.

The build-up of industrial and broadly economic capacity led to the establishment of the first real competing state vehicles in the 1970s and early 1980s. In 1974, the first Singaporean SWF, Temasek, was founded. The initial rationale was to administer the post-independence growth of state ownership in key industries with some distance from policy interference (Chen 2016: 313), while at the same time being "an active investor and shareholder, a forward-looking institution and a trusted steward" (Chen 2013: 3). In order to enable active investment and shareholding, Temasek usually invests not in portfolio stakes but in golden shares or majority stakes in its invested companies. However, its relative distance from political interference by design, and its decidedly commercial mission, bring it closer to the financial strategies discussed in this chapter. Today, Temasek holds just under $300 billion in AuM, which makes it a serious and large peer among the world's sovereign investment vehicles.

In 1981, a second SWF, the Government Investment Corporation (GIC), was founded. Different from Temasek, the GIC is mainly responsible for foreign investment and asset management, and not for administering large-scale state ownership stakes. Its foundation in 1981 was the result of a (political) restructuring of the foreign reserves holding of Singapore (Hamilton-Hart 2000: 198). The GIC is perceived as being under closer government control than Temasek (Chen 2016: 313), not least because it directly manages the state's savings and foreign reserves. The fund holds more than $700 billion in AuM and regularly realizes above average returns on investment. This performance has been described as "legendary" (Shih 2009: 331) in comparison to other SWFs.

After this early formation of some competing state vehicles, Singapore was also among the hard-hit economies of the Asian financial crisis of 1997. However, the experience of the volatility of global financial markets and the vulnerability resulting from Singapore's exposure to these markets did not change its competing state strategy. Rather, the usage of competing state vehicles was understood as an important insurance against post-crisis foreign intervention, for example through international institutional lenders.[7] Through its mixed financial strategy of mostly portfolio, but also golden shares and majority investments, which all generated steady returns on investment, Singapore was able to shake off the losses incurred during the financial crisis. The Singaporean competing state therefore entered the new millennium and a new growth cycle for the East Asian economies well prepared.

Neoliberal globalization as a springboard

While the Singaporean competing state was built up relatively early on, it was not until the heyday of neoliberal globalization that its full potential was unleashed. In the mid-1990s, the net portfolio value of Temasek was below $40 billion, while it grew to almost $300 billion in 2021.[8] Similarly, GIC grew from "several billion dollars" (GIC 2008: 6) invested in the 1980s to $100 billion in 2008 to assets worth over $700 billion today. The success story of these vehicles is closely tied to the increased exploitation of the opportunities neoliberal

7. See Clark and Monk (2010a), who developed this argument in full.
8. Calculated on the basis of self-disclosure by Temasek (2021).

globalization offered. Temasek, for instance, managed to significantly increase its AuM when it started to invest in Asia and later globally in the 2000s. Furthermore, Singaporean government-sponsored vehicles were a major factor beyond the rise of cross-border M&As, where Singapore was the most important non-Organisation for Economic Co-operation and Development (OECD) country between 1990 and 2008 (Goldstein & Pananond 2008: 420). All of this illustrates that the possibilities opening up with the emergence of a transnational agency space were a welcome opportunity for states as owners like Singapore to engage their financial firepower cross-border.

The rise of neoliberal globalization hence represented a fitting springboard for the take-off of the Singaporean competing state. This was even the case against the backdrop of the Asian financial crisis, which generated increasing scepticism regarding the benefits of neoliberal globalization in the region and beyond.[9] Rather than curbing further international integration, Singaporean state-owned vehicles embraced a full going-out strategy after the crisis and anchored the Singaporean competing state in the global economy. Even a recession in mid-2001 did not fundamentally alter this course. This is, for example, reflected in Temasek's strategic reorientation around the early 2000s, when it started to increasingly engage in consolidation efforts, M&As and other forms of strategic behaviour with the goal of becoming a major regional and global investor (Rodan 2004: 486).

Overall, Singapore's competing state capitalized in two ways on the possibilities emerging with neoliberal globalization. First, it extended its reach into cross-border markets and sectors where it acquired know-how and technologies relevant for its SOEs. Via Temasek, the Singaporean competing state acquired stakes in different sectors from banking and finance, to telecoms and real estate, in the 2000s (Goldstein & Pananond 2008: 425). Such a strategy of asset capturing is not typical for pure financial strategies, but rather a sign of a mixed financial strategy as Singapore embraces it. Second, and in higher volumes than regarding the first aspect, Singaporean state-owned vehicles grew their presence in global financial markets via portfolio investment. Here, the GIC in particular played a major role in investing its savings in global equities (about 30 per cent of its portfolio), bonds and cash (about 40 per cent) and other equity forms like real estate (GIC 2021). Different from the Norwegian case, the GIC's investments are both not very transparent and rather illiquid because of their long-term investment character. This again differentiates the Singaporean mixed strategy from other financial strategies. It is clear, however,

---

9. See, for example, Higgott and Phillips (2000) for a discussion of East Asian and Latin American responses to the crises of the late 1990s.

that the GIC portfolio investments serve to generate a long-term, steady flow of revenues to insure the Singaporean economy and society as a sort of "rainy-day fund". Again, different from other financial competing states like the Gulf states, the Singaporean competing state can decidedly *not* draw on natural resources to fund its portfolio investment vehicle (Clark & Monk 2010a: 438). This makes the multidimensional exploitation of the transnational agency space all the more relevant, and it also partly explains the strong exposure to and involvement in global capital circuits as soon as those possibilities for high yields opened up in the 1990s.

Asia and beyond

This exposure and entrance into the global economy took place in (government-) controlled steps. Before the early 2000s, Singaporean cross-border state investment was still mostly found within Asia. While Asia still remains an important destination, the Singaporean competing state also entered other geographical areas; today, for example, almost half of the GIC's portfolio is invested in the USA and Europe, while around a third remains in Asia (GIC 2021). Hence, the geography of the Singaporean competing state changed over time and this expansion made it a global player. Similar to other small states in global markets, Singapore does not embrace a one-sided regional or sectoral strategy, but spreads its investment globally.

This global outreach is visible if we take a look at the overall cross-border investment patterns of the Singaporean state as owner. It is in total invested in 12 out of 14 world regions and 42 other states around the world, with strong ties to Australia, the USA, India, China, the UK and other Asian states like Taiwan, Indonesia and Thailand. The strong ties to former British colonies and dependencies are also rooted in historical legacies, as Singapore itself gained independence from Britain only in 1963. Singapore's global ties entail, among others, majority investments by state-owned telecommunications firms Singtel (under Temasek) and its subsidiaries in Australia, the UK, Japan and South Korea; minority stakes in other telecom firms like Centurylink (USA), retailers like A.S. Watson (China) and global banks like Standard Chartered (UK); and portfolio stakes in large logistics firms like XPO Logistics (USA) and global asset management firms like State Street (USA). This variety of different ownership forms again reflects the mixed financial profile of the Singaporean competing state.

Sector-wise, Singapore differs from other large states as owners with a strong concentration of overseas state capital in telecoms and information technologies (Table 5.2). Other owners, like China, Saudi Arabia and France, focus more on "traditional" sectors like energy supply, manufacturing and mining

Table 5.2 Top-five sectors of Singapore's foreign state investment

Sector	Percentage of total investment
Information and communication	32.1
Manufacturing	22.8
Finance and insurance	18.6
Wholesale and retail	14.2
Transportation and storage	3.8

than Singapore. The focus on information technologies stems from the fact that the Singaporean competing state is built on strong domestic state ownership ties to respective national champions like Singtel. The internationalization of these state-owned champions is one of the key objectives of the transnationalization efforts of the Singaporean competing state (Goldstein & Pananond 2008). Furthermore, investment in manufacturing is mostly conducted via portfolio investment, with some exceptions. The financial and return-driven aspects of Singapore's strategy come to fruition here.

Global, but vulnerable

This geographical and sectoral spread of the Singaporean competing state marks the financial firepower and strong ownership position of another small state in a global economy. At the same time, much of this power is derived from Singapore's liberal statism: the combination of a strong grip of the state on economic and developmental issues in combination with a largely open and FDI-attracting economy. Since Singapore cannot rely on natural resources to fund its competing state, its integration into global circuits of capital, and the absorption and recycling of some of this capital via state-owned vehicles, is vital for its development model. Awareness of this complex situation is also strong among the Singaporean political elite. State-owned institutions like the GIC are, for example, understood as insurance for a natural resource-dependent small economy in a volatile global environment (Clark & Monk 2010a: 439).

However, the openness aspect of this development model is coming increasingly under strain in a changing global order. The tendencies of a so-called deglobalization, or at least "slowbalization" (Linsi 2021), and multilateral efforts to better govern globalization, put development models relying on an open and liberalized global economy under strain. Singapore's liberal statism is one of those models. The country has been described as a so-called conduit offshore financial centre as it channels massive amounts of global investment from origin to destination countries (Garcia-Bernardo *et al.* 2017).

The country gained this status chiefly through its comparatively low income and corporate tax rates that are conducive to global capital. Multilateral efforts to restrict these aspects of a transnational agency space, like the recent OECD agreement on a global minimum corporate tax rate,[10] could become problematic for Singapore's liberal statism. While the agreed minimum corporate tax rate of 15 per cent will not immediately undermine Singapore's low-tax regime, further steps in this direction are likely, with 15 per cent being "a floor" to be increased in the future (US Treasury 2021).

The push for a more regulated and hence shrinking transnational agency space is not only affecting the liberal aspects of Singapore's development model, but also its statist character. In order to be able to maintain its openness based on low tax rates, Singapore's own competing state vehicles – especially its SWFs – are crucial for covering a significant part of total government spending. Through this redistribution mechanism of capital gains to the government household, the Singaporean competing state vehicles have bolstered its low-tax, open economy model for decades (Clark & Monk 2010a). The Singaporean competing state, and especially its returns on investment, hence enable the open Singaporean economy to "survive" low domestic tax rates and its general openness. In a world of decreasing or stalling globalization, it will become increasingly difficult for the country's state-owned investment vehicles to realize the gains necessary to uphold its low-tax development model.

This two-sided pressure from curbed tax competition and a potentially deglobalizing environment forces Singapore's development model, as many others, to adapt. The main question going forward is whether and to what extent the role and form of the Singaporean competing state will be affected by these changes. As has been noticed, even the legitimacy of the Singaporean political system hinges on the ability of state-owned vehicles like Temasek and the GIC to fulfil their stabilizing roles for a fine-tuned but also highly globally dependent and vulnerable Singaporean political economy. Global changes that shrink the transnational agency space available to these vehicles will hence not only affect one aspect of the Singaporean political economy, but could very well lead to cascading effects in the years to come.

In China's shadow?

Another important aspect of the described changes in the global political economy are the ongoing geopolitical shifts affecting the standing of Singapore's

---

10. See OECD (2021) for the agreement among countries covering 90 per cent of global GDP, including Singapore.

competing state. Traditionally, Singapore has acted as a close geopolitical ally of the USA, for example in its so-called war on terror in the 2000s (Rodan 2004: 490). From a global political economy perspective, this alignment meant a broad inclusion and acceptance of Singapore's liberal statist development model in the US-led liberal international order. As described above, Singapore's state-owned foreign investment tools like Temasek and the GIC integrated almost seamlessly into global financial markets in the 1990s and early 2000s. As a small state in South East Asia, this geopolitical alliance was vital for both Singapore's security as well as its economic interests. After all, the USA remains the top source for foreign investment in Singapore (Choong 2021). At the same time, there are strong historical and cultural links to America's major geopolitical rival, China. The majority of Singapore's population are of Chinese descent, and Chinese-born foreigners represent the second largest immigration group in the country (Yang *et al.* 2017: 11). Within the Association of South East Asian Nations, Singapore's role has been interpreted as following a hedging strategy vis-à-vis China, where it balances economic benefits with problematic security issues, for example in the South China Sea (Chen & Yang 2013: 282). Economically, China grew into one of the major partners for Singapore over the last years, for example by becoming one of the main targets of Singaporean foreign investment (Peng Er 2021: 204). This interdependency is also visible from a competing state perspective: China is among the top-five targets for Singaporean state capital, and Singapore receives over 60 per cent of its state-led investment from China.

Over the decades, Singapore hence balanced a mostly friendly and open relationship with an emerging China in tandem with a geopolitical alignment with the USA. However, with China's rise as a potential contender to US hegemony and the "new Cold War", ambivalent geopolitical alignments become more problematic. Singapore's current strategic position has aptly been described as a "small state caught between giants" (Peng Er 2021: 204). This is not only a security issue, but also has consequences for the standing of the Singaporean competing state. As I have argued above, Singapore's state-owned vehicles are not only an important insurance mechanism for economic turbulence, but constitute the backbone of the country's development model. In a world where at least partial decoupling of US and Chinese value chains, economic sanctions and new rivalries are being fought out globally, this backbone could come under serious strain. After all, Singapore's globally active investment vehicles rely on Western, and especially US, markets, which are the top destination for Singapore's state-led portfolio investment. Curbing or even shutting down this investment channel would have serious consequences for the survival outlook of Singapore's competing state.

A foretaste of these problems has been the USA–China trade war starting in 2018. After various rounds of tit-for-tat economic sanctions, Singapore was estimated to be among the main countries suffering losses in global value chains (Wu *et al.* 2021: 11). A strong economic contraction in the second half of 2019 led to worries on the side of the Singaporean political elite.[11] Singapore's prime minister even wrote an op-ed expressing his concerns over disrupted supply chains, issues with R&D financing and other economic problems resulting from the trade war (Loong 2019). The fallout of the China–USA standoff was soon also felt by the Singaporean competing state vehicles. Alarmed and worried by the development of the trade war, the GIC shifted some of its investments to emerging economies like Vietnam that were profiting from Chinese production relocations (CNBC 2019). Similarly, Temasek's returns for 2019 were negatively impacted by the trade war, leading it to redirect large parts of its investments to unlisted, and thus potentially less trade war-exposed, firms (Iwamoto 2019). The effects of intensifying global rivalries, and the delicate geopolitical position of Singapore in those, has thus concrete effects on its competing state profitability and behaviour. Such developments are unlikely to be of a temporary nature, as the tensions between the USA and China did not significantly ease under the new Biden administration.

Is the future of the Singaporean competing state to be pulverized in new rounds of global rivalries between geopolitical superpowers? This might be a less probable outlook, as the trade war episode suggests. It is on the one hand likely that the role of state-led investment will be more scrutinized and politicized in a post-neoliberal era. This is especially the case for geopolitically sensitive cases like Singapore and its liberal statist model. On the other hand, the Singaporean competing state has proven to be relatively resilient to major crises and uncertainties in the last three decades. Similar to other financial strategies, it invests long term and draws on a diversified portfolio that guarantees a continuous revenue stream for the Singaporean development model. Despite global political distortions, neither of the two competing superpowers indicated that Singapore will be forced to pick sides in the near future. And even the mentioned difficulties of Singapore's investment vehicles amid the trade war are not absolute: despite the trade war, Singaporean investment in Chinese real estate reached new heights in 2019 (Ren 2019). For the USA, Temasek announced that it remains a long-term investment target with or without trade war tensions.[12] Consequently, the Singaporean competing state, and in extension its liberal statist development model, could prove more resilient than the currently emerging global rivalries and geopolitical fissures suggest.

---

11. See Lee (2019) for reactions by the Singaporean trade minister.
12. See the announcement by Temasek in Straits Times (2019).

6

Consequences: Covid-19, geoeconomics and climate change

The previous chapters have unpacked the rise of the state as a global economic owner over recent decades, described the historical and structural circumstances of this rise and analysed several important cases. This chapter takes a broader perspective and asks questions about the future of the competing state in a world in flux. I divide the chapter into three sections. The first section deals with the *short-term* consequences of competing state politics after the Covid-19 pandemic that started in late December 2019. The pandemic not only had devastating human and social consequences but is also reshuffling the political-economic coordinates of many industrialized and emerging economies around the world. The role of state capital is in many instances at the heart of these discussions: what role will state-led investment play in the rebuilding and transformation of growth models and the global political economy as such?

The second section deals with the *medium term* and the role and function of state capital in the intensifying global rivalries that will define the 2020s. The rise of China and the hegemonic struggles this rise initiated with the USA and Europe are of a different nature than previous cycles of global rivalries: they are often not fought out in purely geopolitical, but in predominantly geoeconomic, terms. State capital, as a source of investment and economic power, is increasingly being scrutinized in this respect, for example as a potential "state capitalist" threat for developed economies. The question here is whether and how state-led investment will be weaponized in these power struggles, and what this weaponization might look like.

The third section dives into the *long-term* issue of climate change, its mitigation and the role of different state investment forms for such mitigation strategies. Although the immediate pressure for rapid decarbonization is high and should be taken more seriously in political and academic debates, climate change mitigation requires a long-term strategic outlook to be successful. Beyond the electoral cycle in which the pandemic is dealt with, or the decade-defining new geoeconomic rivalries, climate change and its politics will govern the rest of the century in important ways. I argue that the role of the state as an economic owner, and the resulting decarbonization potentials, have so far been understudied and represent an important building block for effective, long-term decarbonization strategies.

Covid-19 and the political economy of "state comebacks"

A pandemic is, from a historical perspective, nothing entirely new: cities, states, regions and in some cases also the entire world have suffered pandemics and plagues throughout the centuries. From a political economy perspective, however, the Covid-19 pandemic is in many ways unprecedented. It is, for instance, the first pandemic in an extremely densely connected and globalized world, which makes local containment impossible and its global suppression necessary. While previous pandemics also had a global character, Covid-19 stands out as the first pathogen to conquer the whole globe in mere months. Despite strict lockdown measures around the world, there were basically no world regions by mid-2020 where Covid-19 did not occur or cause an outbreak. Furthermore, the depth and gravity of the economic impact of this pandemic outstrips previous health and economic crises by far. Over 100 million people could slip into extreme poverty, causing this rate to grow instead of an expected decline in 2021 (World Bank 2020). Likewise, over 100 million people are estimated to have either lost their employment or shifted to economic inactivity in 2020 (ILO 2021). On top of this, a stunning 3.3 billion people were under a furlough scheme at different points in 2020, which reflects an unheard-of contraction of the global economy in just a few weeks (Tooze 2021). In addition to these social factors, the global economy itself suffered from one of the steepest declines in growth rates ever measured, in combination with a growing debt burden, especially in the Global South (Blake & Wadhwa 2020). Overall, the pandemic at least fundamentally distorted, and in many aspects outright devastated, different sectors and spheres of the global political economy.

This unprecedented economic downturn in 2020 soon raised political questions: who would pay for the emerging economic burden? Which sectors, groups and actors would profit from a reset of the global economy post-Covid? Which lessons are to be learned for economic policy-making, disaster preparedness and the overall resilience of economies and societies? One common theme among those hotly debated questions was the role of the state.

In the midst of an unprecedented slowdown in global markets in the spring of 2020, political attention turned to the nation state. As in 2008, many states around the world mobilized vast sums of capital to save their economies, for example through the suspension of fiscal rules, deferral of tax and other payments, company loans, furlough compensation schemes, one-time payments for lockdown-induced profit losses, extended social and sick leave payments and other forms of support for firms and citizens. The IMF estimates that states like the USA spent up to a quarter of their GDP on fiscal measures related to the Covid-19 pandemic until mid-2021 (IMF 2021). In some instances, like in Germany or France, governments even extended their ownership stakes in troubled sectors like the airline industry and nationalized firms. In total, the fiscal and other state-related financial measures exceed the post-2008 crisis efforts by far[1].

This (fiscal) omnipotence of many high-income states led observers to ask the question of whether we are witnessing a "return of the state" (Kundnani 2020), while others were demanding such a return to ensure an equitable post-crisis recovery. Organizations like the European Bank for Reconstruction and Development (EBRD) even place the Covid-induced state activity in a longer process of a "striking back" of the state after neoliberal globalization (EBRD 2020). Different from the post-2008 landscape, a swift return to post-crisis austerity policies seems less viable in a post-Covid and pre-climate catastrophe world. Massive state-led investment, as envisaged by the new Biden administration in the USA and progressive political forces around the world, is evaluated as a key policy tool to meet both crises that will govern the 2020s. The different competing states are, from a first look, in a good position to become important instruments in this endeavour. After all, state-owned vehicles like Singapore's Temasek, GIC and its central bank together channelled almost $40 billion of their reserves into Covid-related fiscal measures (GIC 2021: 7), while others like Saudi Arabia's Public Investment Fund (PIF) took advantage of the Covid-induced low asset prices and went on a global "shopping spree" in the USA and elsewhere (England & Massoudi 2020). However, as attractive as "state comeback" narratives are, they need to be scrutinized against real-world developments, especially when it comes to specific phenomena like state-led investment. In the following, I delineate how I believe the Covid-19 crisis will impact the further trajectory of the competing state. I argue that we should be more precise in what we mean when we speak of state comebacks and returns. This can help in developing an empirically grounded political economy of so-called state comebacks, be it in fiscal, ownership or political hindsight.

---

1. For an early comparison between 2008 and 2020 see, for example, Strauss-Kahn (2020).

Of pendulums and comebacks

In Chapter 2, I discussed what I dubbed a "popularized Polanyi-ism" that often shapes periodical discussions about so-called state comebacks or returns. A variant of this perspective is "Polanyi's pendulum". It takes Polanyi's original model of the double movement and extends it to be an invisible force governing the history of market societies. The core claim of this basic model is that market societies regularly swing between "market domination" and "restrictions on the market" when the former tendency leads to excesses (Stewart 2010). This "pendular" refunctioning of Polanyi's thesis (Dale 2012: 5) gained increased popular and academic attention and usage after 2008 (see King 2017; Gills 2008). The expectation of many observers was that the excesses of neoliberal globalization, especially on overleveraged financial markets, would push the pendulum back to market restrictions by empowered governments (Skidelsky 2009). However, the following wave of austerity politics in Europe and elsewhere demonstrated rather the opposite: the fusion of state power with disciplinary instruments from the neoliberal playbook indicates that the interplay of market excess and state "comebacks" is more complex than Polanyi's pendulum suggests. For state capital in particular, we saw in previous chapters of this book how it was the sweeping rise of neoliberal globalization itself that created the possibility for the competing state to develop in the first place. Market expansion thus prepared the ground for state vehicles to rise as global owners. While being an elegant summary of the inherent difficulties in governing market societies, a pendular reading of the effect of Covid-19 on the "comeback of the state" would probably just scratch the surface of what we should expect the 2020s to look like for existing competing states.

In order to build a more robust and precise political economy of state comebacks, I suggest three core elements which are also reflected in recent (critical) political economy research. First, we need to distinguish clearly between different state apparatuses and state fractions when analysing the rise and demise of state activity. Work drawing on (critical) state theory, such as the Gramscian tradition or power resource theory, provides a more realistic understanding of states as complex institutional ensembles (Block 2008; Hameiri & Jones 2016; Weiss 2003). States are in this regard not unitary actors, but consist of various institutions and apparatuses that can in some instances be quite autonomous in relation to each other. This autonomy also influences diagnoses of state comebacks: SWFs have, for instance, been analysed in this tradition as a major locus of growing state power under changing parameters of neoliberal globalization.[2] As I argued in Chapter 1, the rise of state capital and its investment vehicles is an example *par excellence* of a "rise" of a specific type of state apparatus but not others.

These insights lead to the second relevant point, namely a differentiation not only of state apparatuses but also of varying state *roles*. In neoclassical economic theory, and related strands of more applied economic policy thinking, the role of the state is often confined to a non-interventionist one that only sets and supervises the rules of the game. From a critical political economy perspective, states and state apparatuses engage in much more than rule-setting: they are responsible, to varying degrees, for market creation, correction, direction and external representation of domestic capital (van Apeldoorn *et al.* 2012: 474). Different states take on these roles via different channels and vehicles. Whereas authoritarian state forms centralize political and economic authority in a command-and-control manner, others delegate this authority and control to other agencies, sometimes even outside the formal institutional state architecture. "Returns" of the state are in this reading rather a rearrangement of different state roles vis-à-vis the economy over time. The rise of transnational state investment falls under the category of an increased market direction arising out of the surpluses generated by (resource-rich) states and the possibilities the emerging transnational agency space offers for recycling these surpluses.

A third important element is to introduce a historically more sensitive understanding of state comebacks. Different from a pendular understanding, the rise and fall of statism takes place in historically specific circumstances. I suggested such a historically sensitive reading of the rise of statism in the global economy in Chapter 2 of this book. This periodization builds on the notion of "waves" of historical state activity introduced by Andreas Nölke (Nölke 2014). Furthermore, recent work on "state capitalism" suggested and introduced a historically more grounded understanding of how, when and under which circumstances states rise as economic actors (Alami & Dixon 2020a). For foreign state investment, this means an orientation towards the different instruments through which, the geographies into which and the global environments within which state capital is rising.

With these three elements it is possible to tackle the question of the role of state capital during and after the global Covid-19 crisis. We do not need to fall back on generalized ideas about the "return" of the state or imprecise pendulum metaphors. Rather, we can bring more analytical precision to the

---

2. Weiss (2012) discussed SWFs in this respect, calling out the "myth" of the neoliberal state.

discussion about the effects of the pandemic on how competing states may or may not profit from its economic fallout. As an example, the increased security and surveillance powers certain state factions received out of the need to control the spread of the virus does not necessarily translate into increased state power across the board. Similarly, the failure of some aspects of the "neoliberal regulatory state"[3] does not imply that state legitimacy in other areas of social life has suffered similarly. The following analysis takes these considerations on board for assessing the effect of Covid-19 on the future of global competing states. I divide the analysis between financial and controlling strategies as I did previously.

Financial strategies: rainy days and shopping trips

Financial competing state strategies emerge for a variety of reasons and are employed for different goals. One of the overarching motives of states investing their savings portfolios is to have a national version of a "rainy-day fund". What constitutes a rainy day can vary; it can, for instance, mean a quarterly recession, a longer structural transformation of the economy or a pandemic-induced economic crisis. The latter hit many financially oriented competing states in early 2020, when the Covid-induced global shutdowns and other precautionary measures put a strain on economies and government budgets. Consequently, many competing states with the respective financial firepower stepped in to stabilize government budgets. Until September 2020, the estimated mobilized sum of sovereign and other national investment vehicles hit the $100 billion threshold, which is expected to rise further (Arnold 2020). States like Norway or Singapore took massive sums out of their SWFs to cover unexpected crisis expenses. Next to stabilizing government expenditures, many sovereign vehicles engaged in direct support for troubled or promising domestic companies: Singapore's Temasek stabilized its national airline with almost $9 billion, and the Russian Direct Investment Fund almost single-handedly financed the development of the Sputnik V vaccine (Clark 2021). In sum, sovereign portfolio investment instruments played a crucial role for their domestic economies in the first critical weeks and months of the pandemic.

This inward turn was, at the same time, only possible after many years in which those competing states have been exposed to global markets. The participation in, and exploitation of, the transnational agency space was especially successful for states adapting a financial strategy. Investment vehicles

---

3. See Jones and Hameiri (2021) for an analysis of Covid-19 and neoliberal regulatory state failures.

like Norway's GPF-G went into 2020 with enormous returns on investment and a portfolio of more than $1 trillion in AuM. The decade before the pandemic was extremely successful for other portfolio competing states, such as the Gulf states: in total, global SWFs alone roughly doubled their AuM from about $4 trillion in 2010 to almost $8 trillion in 2019 (SWFI 2019). This success story of transnationally invested state capital prepared these states to provide domestic stabilization when the Covid-19 pandemic hit. Different from other advanced economies, which had to engage in deficit spending, most often by taking on new government debt, competing states could simply reroute money from their large investment funds. This possibility not only increased the independence of states from external creditors, but also reduced potential societal conflicts about which social groups have to carry the financial burden after the pandemic.

The outwards orientation of many financial competing states also continued unabated throughout the pandemic. When global asset valuations spiralled downwards, Saudi Arabia's PIF vehicle took advantage of cheap share prices and bought into, for example, large cruise ship operators, hotel chains and live event organizers in the spring of 2020.[4] Forced by plunging asset prices, Norwegian investments in similar US stock market-listed companies increased in the same time period.[5] This active exploitation of the "Covid dip" in global markets also extended to biotechnology, where state-led investment grew again in 2020 and 2021 after a low in 2019 (SWFI 2021). State-owned vehicles from Qatar, the UAE or Singapore continue to engage in cross-border investment to either compete for future returns on investment or to secure a stake in the development of relevant biotech knowledge for future pandemics and medical breakthroughs. These sovereign investment strategies are unlikely to be fundamentally rewritten because of Covid-19, especially when it comes to their transnational orientation.

Notwithstanding this diagnosis, one caveat remains: sovereign investment vehicles have been much more inwards oriented than in the GFC, which brought them to a global stage in 2008. Back then, it was especially SWFs from Asia and the Middle East that "saved" troubled US financial institutions through their equity investments (Helleiner & Lundblad 2008). During the Covid-19 crisis, many states used the reserves and the liquidity that had been

---

4. PIF bought a stake in Live Nation (events), Marriott International (hotels) and Carnival (cruise operator), among others, in early 2020 (England & Massoudi 2020; IFSWF 2021).
5. The Norwegian SWF had to buy additional stakes in firms like Live Nation due to their dropping share prices in order to keep the SWF portfolio in balance: it is required to hold about 70 per cent in equities, which was endangered by lower asset prices due to Covid-19 (Weiss & Holter 2020).

built up since 2008 to stabilize their domestic economies.[6] The vast majority of investment in 2020 was indeed used for such stabilization measures in the broadest sense. This raises the question of whether financial competing states are going through a watershed moment that will transform the logic of their strategy. Instead of accumulating reserves by investing in promising global equities, many investment vehicles might find themselves involved in domestic affairs more directly than beforehand. This is especially the case for strongly globally oriented funds like the GIC, which were not designed as typical stabilization funds. In an era of increased uncertainty and potentially less global investment opportunities, formerly "global" funds could orient themselves more towards domestic affairs. This would not simply mean a reorientation, but a transformation of the economic and political role of financial competing states. While the political discussions around those competing states were for a long time confined to finding the "right" outwards strategy, future discussions could involve more controversies about the right amount and strategy of domestic investment. Different domestic players and fractions will vie for this rerouted sovereign capital, which could create new distribution conflicts between the winners and losers of this redistribution.

Controlling strategies: the end of expansion?

For competing states that employ controlling strategies, Covid-19 brought about a different but related set of problems. Different from financial competing states, controlling strategies have much less liquid capital at their command. This means that filling government budget holes, offsetting fiscal deficits or directly supporting ailing industries via state-owned means are much harder to accomplish for these competing states. On the contrary, because of plummeting oil prices in the first phase of the pandemic, many state-owned fossil fuel companies had to be supported by their government sponsors. Russia, for example, relieved its oil-producing SOEs from production target fines, included them in financial support schemes and proposed an emergency fund for unfinished wells (Shagina 2020). In the Middle East, North Africa and Central Asia, SOEs have not significantly contributed to rising pandemic costs, but on the contrary made use of government funds and support to uphold their operations, among others (Olugbade *et al.* 2021: 74). On top of this, some fossil-exporting states and their SOEs have engaged in so-called resource-backed loans in recent years. This type of loan agreement envisages a repayment either in natural resources or the income streams derived from

---

6. See IFSWF (2021) for a similar argument and further examples.

these resources (Mihalyi *et al.* 2020). The opacity of these agreements makes them a high-risk loan agreement form, which becomes especially problematic during a global pandemic and dropping prices for commodities such as oil (OECD 2020: 7). In sum, states that invest predominantly in majority stakes in firms could tend to rely less on those assets as rainy-day insurance, but in many cases had to lend financial support to these companies.

However, whereas these phenomena certainly put a strain on the ability to expand controlling strategies further, they have to be differentiated. First, most of the additional debt burden, or financial support by home governments, is targeted at domestically oriented SOEs and the crucial roles they fulfil for their respective economies. As an example, in the above-mentioned cases, the surveyed governments claimed that job protection, the functioning of public services, the support for growth and strategic assets protection were the over-arching motives for additional SOE support (Olugbade *et al.* 2021: 75). This only has an indirect effect on competing state strategies, such as through the redirection of funds to the domestic economy. Second, most of the large and powerful competing states surveyed in this book have the means to absorb the Covid-19 shock for their SOEs, sometimes even with other investment vehicles.[7] The fact that many controlling strategies do not enable states to cover pandemic-induced budget deficits does not mean that these states cannot take up additional debt or find other ways of shouldering this burden. As such, the effect of Covid-19 on competing states is in this respect not uniform, and most large states with controlling strategies, such as China or France, managed to shield their assets from the economic fallout.

Besides these fiscal aspects, a second development exacerbated by the pandemic will have a major effect on controlling strategies. During the early stages of Covid-19, states around the world introduced stricter measures for screening and evaluating inwards FDI (Caon 2020). The main concern, especially of large and industrialized economies, was that downward-spiralling asset prices in early 2020 could invite hostile takeovers of domestic firms by foreign actors. Foreign state-owned or state-directed entities received particular attention from policy-makers. In this regard, the European Commission, for instance, issued guidelines to "protect critical European assets" through investment screening as laid out in its FDI screening regulations from 2019, which explicitly relates to "state entities" as one FDI source to be scrutinized (EU Commission 2020). Some states, like Germany or the UK, entered this situation coming out of a recent history of disputes about the role of (Chinese)

---

7. Exemplary here are the Gulf competing states, which often own large state-owned oil multinationals and sovereign investment vehicles at the same time.

foreign state-led investment and takeovers of domestic firms (Babic & Dixon 2022). The pre-Covid situation hence already presented a challenge for many competing states, as controlling strategies rely heavily on majority-owned SOEs abroad, including brownfield and greenfield FDI conducted by these states. With the disruptions caused by Covid-19, these protectionist tendencies have only been accelerated: investment screening evolved "from a nice subject to a broader regulatory tool that touches an expanding share of global economic activity" (Gertz 2021). Controlling strategies are already being affected negatively by these developments, as recent blockades of state-backed takeover attempts in Germany and elsewhere demonstrate (see Bauerle Danzman & Meunier 2021).

What does the Covid-19 pandemic mean for the rebuilding and future of different political economies in general, and competing states in particular? As we have seen, the pandemic is having and will continue to have differentiated effects on the future of various competing states in the global political economy. For financial strategies, the pandemic was a stress test that in many instances proved the value of owning a fund able to cover unforeseen expenses. Previously accumulated state capital and the new state involvement in the economy appeared to be a positive development that absorbed much of the worst consequences of the largest economic downturn in decades. For controlling strategies, the fact that many SOEs needed additional financial support and the accelerated adaptation of investment screening mechanisms herald a new phase of fewer investment opportunities. States that have a reputation for being "statist" or "state capitalist" have felt the changed global investment climate particularly strongly, as exemplified by China and Russia. For rebuilding political economies and development models after the crisis, this differentiation has had important consequences: a focus on expanding controlling strategies could in the medium run lead to a dead end in which a protectionist global economy translates into a shrinking agency space for such strategies. State-led takeovers and majority investments are today, and especially after the pandemic, a delicate and hotly debated issue for policy-makers around the world. There are not many indications that these increased tensions will be reduced in the years ahead of us.

With this analysis, we can also draw a more nuanced conclusion for the question of whether Covid-19 means a state comeback from a state capital perspective. First, the pandemic did bring back generalized discussions about the need for more state intervention in the global political economy. Some of the developments we observed with regards to financialized strategies indicate that states as owners could play a more important role in a post-pandemic world. Large state-owned pools of capital could be considered an important insurance mechanism in the insecure and volatile global political economy we are likely to see in the 2020s. At the same time, we can also expect a retraction or at least a stagnation of the further expansion of large-scale state-led takeovers in the global economy if the introduced protectionist measures are more than temporary adjustments. The pandemic laid bare the exposure of vital domestic assets and the potential vulnerability of some states in an open transnational agency space where powerful, state-backed actors are able to exploit distressed asset prices, for instance through takeovers. The "comeback" of the state could hence take a different form and different logic from the one we would expect for financial strategies. A political economy of state comebacks should take into account these important nuances in order to better understand the complex post-Covid world into which the global political economy is moving. The next section takes this analysis as a starting point and explores the medium-run effects of a changing global order for state capital transnationalization.

Geoeconomics and a changing (neo)liberal order

Developments like the discussed intensification of investment screening mechanisms are pandemic-induced, but have a longer history that for some started after the GFC of 2008.[8] From another perspective, it is the phase after 2015, with the rise of Trumpism, a more assertive China and a more "geopolitical" Europe, which is transforming the international environment gradually. As a result, the global political economy of today looks quite different – more protectionist and even more hostile – than after the last global economic crisis. Such developments are especially problematic for state-owned investment vehicles. The previous section demonstrated that the transnational agency space is at least becoming less attractive for state-led investment, and that it even shrinks for some forms of state capital in the short run because of the Covid-19 pandemic. In this section, I analyse what this development implies for the medium run in a global political economy of renewed global rivalries and hegemonic transitions.

Scholars and observers of world politics have used different terms to describe the new phase of global politics that begun around 2015–16. From a global political economy perspective, the concept of an emerging "geoeconomic order" seems particularly useful (Roberts *et al.* 2019). Anthea Roberts and colleagues introduced this concept to capture the transition away from what they dub a post-Cold War "neoliberal order" that shaped global economic

---

8. See, for example, Bauerle Danzman and Meunier (2021), who date the rising interest in investment screening to the phase after 2008.

relations since the early 1990s. Different from the neoliberal order, the emerging geoeconomic world would, in this reading, re-emphasize questions of national security in and through economic relations. Global economic relations hence move away "from an emphasis on cooperation to one of competition and conflict" (Roberts *et al.* 2019: 5) Similarly, other contributions in the field emphasize the competitive character of the emerging geoeconomic order and the reappreciation of "economic statecraft" in this regard (Babic *et al.* 2022; Gertz & Evers 2020). Others have used slightly different wording – such as the "geopoliticization" of trade and investment (Meunier & Nicolaidis 2019) – pointing out essentially the same trend in global economic relations.

This stark contrast between a "neoliberal" and a "geoeconomic" order is certainly a conceptual simplification. Economic statecraft, for example in the form of tariffs, strategic support of national champions or outright economic warfare, also took place before 2016. At the same time, the notion of the advent of a more competitive and conflictual global economic environment within the crisis of neoliberal globalization is a useful *analytical* distinction. The assumption of a more "geoeconomic" world carries with it the insight that some of the latent defects of neoliberal globalization – such as large macroeconomic imbalances between different economies in the eurozone, the exploding current account deficit of the USA, increasing environmental devastation or rising inequality within and between economies – over a longer period of relative calm slowly morph into a more conflictive environment. The political and economic decline of the USA as a fragile hegemon and the rise of China as its prime challenger adds to this incremental transformation of the global political economy.

For analysing the rise of state capital, the distinction between a past phase of neoliberal globalization and an emerging phase of geoeconomic competition is quite instructive. As described in the preceding chapters, the rise of state capital in the global economy is the product of decades of neoliberal globalization. Only through the transnational agency space that emerged in the course of global neoliberal restructuring has state-led investment had the chance to thrive as yet another form of productive capital in the global economy. With the advent of a more competitive and conflictive global environment, the nature of states as the owners and investors of state capital came into focus: "state capitalism" became a shorthand for a suspicious and even malicious type of actor that used SOEs and SWFs as instruments in a systemic competition with Western-style liberal capitalism (Kurlantzick 2016). Previously overlooked state-owned investment vehicles became a topic in discourses about the rise of China and other emerging economies in the world system. A strong tendency in these discussions is to treat "state capitalism" as a geopolitical category "which acts as a powerful tool in categorizing and hierarchizing the spaces of world politics"

(Alami & Dixon 2020b). This tendency only increases in a world that is becoming more geoeconomic, where distributional conflicts are also fought out on a discursive level.

This production of a hierarchical and dichotomizing discourse is certainly problematic for many competing states. A large number of competing states that employ investment vehicles cross-border are also considered to be "state capitalist" economies in common classifications.[9] Being branded "state capitalist" in a geoeconomic world does not help many of those states to avoid additional scrutiny and political backlash when they seek to engage in cross-border investment.

However, besides these discursive aspects, a geoeconomic world also holds new *material* barriers for the engagement of competing states in the global economy. One major development in recent years is the previously mentioned introduction of investment screening mechanisms across the developed world. Countries like the USA, Germany, the UK and France have either installed new mechanisms or tightened existing ones in recent years. Many of these new mechanisms are specifically targeting "state-based" entities that seek to invest in the domestic economy and thereby possibly gain control of important companies or nodes in value chains as foreign state powers. It is especially China, and its state-led investment forms, that drive much of the increasing protectionism vis-à-vis state capital on a global scale (Babic & Dixon 2022).

There are in principle two main ways in which investment screening regimes can be tightened: either via the lowering or total abolition of investment thresholds, or via the extension of screening mechanisms to more sectors than the ones that are crucial for national security (such as military equipment or critical infrastructure). Both forms have different consequences for different competing states. The first measure is especially problematic for financial strategies, whose portfolio investments can become part of investment screening procedures when thresholds are lowered or abolished. The second measure is problematic for controlling strategies that used to invest in non-security-related sectors and with the extension of targeted sectors that might become subject to investment screening. Either way, the raising of (soft) protectionist measures implies a shrinking of the transnational agency space for state capital across the globe.

If we accept the diagnosis that the new geoeconomic world emerging out of the rubble of neoliberal globalization will become a more hostile environment

---

9. See, for example, Kurlantzick (2016: 14), who uses a list of around 20 countries he classifies as state capitalist, among which are powerful competing states such as China, Russia, Saudi Arabia and Singapore.

for state capital in the next decade or so, we need ways of studying this phenomenon on a global scale. Next to governance-related issues such as investment screening or other protectionist measures, this involves first and foremost a good understanding of *where* and *how* states are invested in the global economy, and where investment concentration could possibly lead to geoeconomic competition and conflict. If state capital is a transnational phenomenon, and if the emerging geoeconomic order is posing new challenges to state-led investment forms, we need to develop a global understanding of its destinations and the possible reverberations that stem from this investment.

What does state capital do in a geoeconomic world?

Understanding where state investment could possibly cause political reverberations and also pushbacks requires a perspective that takes the geoeconomic nature of state-led investment seriously. When we speak about the targets of state-led investment, we often tend to think in dyads, that is, in terms of state-to-state investment relations. State A investing in state B is a convenient and straightforward way of describing how state capital moves within the global political economy. Such a perspective is also common outside the particular realm of foreign state investment, for example when we look at typical macroeconomic indicators like the IMF balance of payments statistics.[10] The global political economy that such a perspective describes is an international space in the truest sense of the word: it consists of different national entities that invest in each other via state-owned vehicles. The political economy of foreign state investment should consequently take an international rather than a transnational perspective.

Such an understanding of the senders and targets of state capital has some benefits. For instance, it enables us to carve out and compare the varying strategies of states as cross-border investors. It also allows for a straightforward way of describing where this state capital is flowing to. If the targets of foreign state investment are other states, it is quite simple to determine "who gets what" and which international political reverberations could stem from this investment. I dub this perspective a *geopolitical reading* of foreign state-led investment. The potential conflicts emerging out of the creation of state-to-state ties are to be found in the dynamics between those states. For example, if a state decides to buy a firm or to set up a state-owned subsidiary in another state, the host state of this investment could become suspicious about the true motives of

---

10. For the problems arising out of dyadic and "international" statistics in times of globalization see Linsi and Mügge (2019).

this investment: is it to dominate the domestic market of the host, to transfer a specific technology, to control a potential world market competitor or simply a commercial transaction? Recent research confirms that some host states have reservations about SOEs from other countries rising as global investors and owners (Cuervo-Cazurra 2018). The geopolitical reading, in a nutshell, takes these issues seriously and understands foreign state investment as a potential projection of state power abroad through economic means (Babic 2021).

The geopolitical reading also has some bearing in reality, if we think of cases like Russia's Gazprom and its role in Russia's cooperation and conflicts with the EU over the last decades. The relationship between (state-owned and other) firms in these settings has been described as a "direct source of geopolitical outcomes" (Abdelal 2015: 553). Despite their profit orientation, firms and investments can become part of geopolitical means and ends in specific geopolitical setting. This is especially the case for state-owned firms and vehicles. The role Gazprom and Rosneft and their managerial elites play in the 2022 assault on Ukraine and the subsequent sanctions regime against Russia are a case in point. On the other hand, cases like these are not the standard mode of operation of state capital across borders. As I argued in previous chapters, state-led investment usually follows broadly economic motives when it aims to reap the benefits of a globalized economy. The exploitation of the transnational agency space means the usage and leverage of economic structures and incentives. The fact that state capital can move more or less freely within this space is closely connected to the fact that it most often aims to mimic its private peers, especially when it comes to financial competing state strategies (Clark *et al.* 2013; Liu & Dixon 2021).

If the majority of foreign state-led investment is decidedly not employed to facilitate geopolitical goals, how can we think about state capital in a geoeconomic world? Taking the emergence of a more geoeconomic global political economy seriously, we cannot simply assume that state capital is nothing but a commercial enterprise either. Think about the introduction of investment screening mechanisms against "state-based threats" across many developed economies, the role of China which is perceived as the emergence of a muscular "state capitalism" or the heated political discussions about SOEs as potential sources of threat, especially during the Covid-induced fragility of many European economies.[11] State capital is not just another commercial phenomenon, and its investment cross-border is causing political reverberations. While competing states are often not geopolitically motivated per se, the global quest

---

11. See the recent discussions about the possible intervention of EU states into domestic companies to fend off Chinese state capitalist competition (Espinoza 2020).

for assets and profits creates competitive and potentially conflictive patterns and consequences for the global political economy.

I describe this emerging politics of foreign state investment as *geoeconomic competition*. Through their investment behaviour in a shrinking transnational agency space, states can and often do create political reverberations. These can stem, for example, from the competition for similar investment targets with other (state-led or private) investors. Similarly, regulatory, political and economic conflicts with the host governments of state-led investment are a source of potential competition. Finally, competition with other states over the domination of, or the market infrastructure in, a third state are conceivable, such as the recent confrontations between the US and Chinese governments over the provision of 5G infrastructure in other parts of the world. Taken together, state-led investment can and does lead to geoeconomic competition and conflict that is not primarily geopolitical. Geoeconomic reverberations rather stem from the pursuit of economic motives broadly speaking: the search for returns on investment; attempts at asset capture, technology transfer or knowledge acquisition via state investment; control of critical infrastructures, important niche suppliers or important nodes in global value chains; and other forms and motivations for cross-border state investment.

This type of geoeconomic competition is different from the geopolitical reading for a number of reasons. For one, it does not assume the global political economy to be an international space populated by unitary acting nation states. Rather, the geoeconomic perspective emphasizes the *transnational* nature of the global agency space into which different economic and political actors can move. Phenomena like global value chains or production networks are not simply nationally contained, but cross borders and different scales from the local to the global. The global political economy, in which states rise as owners, is a complex system that cannot be reduced to the existence of other states in the system (Oatley 2019). Recent scholarship in IPE and International Relations (IR) has demonstrated how a complexity approach has explanatory power in a world dominated by transnational economic networks, which fundamentally reshape the nation state-centric logic of international politics and economic competition.[12] Another important aspect following from such a geoeconomic perspective is that the *targets* of foreign state investment are not simply other states. States as owners invest in concrete companies, which are located in concrete sectors. Assuming that they conduct this investment simply to project power into another state would be reductionist at best. Instead,

---

12. For the emerging complexity-perspective in IR and IPE see especially Farrell & Newman (2019), Oatley (2019) and Winecoff (2020).

turning our attention to the *real* targets of foreign state investment can help us to better determine its concrete dynamics "on the ground". As an example, take the largest Chinese outwards FDI transaction ever. The $40 billion acquisition of Swiss Syngenta in 2017 was certainly not primarily a geopolitical move by China to project power into Switzerland. Rather, the transaction was meant to bring Chinese agricultural production and research up to date and to increase the competitiveness of Chinese SOEs in the global seeds business. Similarly, most state-led acquisitions and investments at least aim for economic goals, be they asset acquisition or profit generation.

Elsewhere,[13] I have developed a methodological tool to map and analyse the concentration of cross-border state capital. This method builds on the premise that we should look at sectors and their regional composition instead of at states as targets of foreign state investment. The reasons for this methodological choice lie in the nature of the global political economy sketched above: in the era of cross-border value and wealth chain organization, of transnational production and exchange, and of cross-border networked production regimes, it does not make sense to fall back on a state-centric reading of foreign state investment.[14] Likewise, focusing only on firms as targets of this investment would not be helpful, as this would lead to an isolated treatment of single investment ties and not provide a systemic overview. Focusing on cross-border sectoral investment patterns instead is not only justified from a theoretical perspective, but also bolstered by reality. For instance, Chinese state-led acquisitions in the course of realizing its MiC strategy deliberately targeted not specific *firms* but specific *sectors* (Wübbeke *et al.* 2016). Likewise, competing states with financial strategies also target specific sectors, geographical areas and other macro-variables – or follow existing indices – rather than picking specific firms to invest in.

Following this method, I dub the emerging units of analysis *geoindustrial clusters*. They consist of a combination of regional geographic information and industry classifications that allow me to analyse large datasets with many investment ties that have information on these two and other variables. These geoindustrial clusters are certainly only one way of aggregating cross-border state capital and mapping its global outreach. However, they represent an empirical access point to better understand how state capital is concentrated globally. Moreover, this concentration is not restricted to the national scale, but allows us to detect global cross-border patterns of industrial and sectoral

---

13. For the respective method and global mapping of foreign state investment see Babic (2021).

14. For some of the relevant literature see Coe *et al.* (2008) and Henderson *et al.* (2002).

Table 6.1 Global investment of cross-border state capital by top-ten sectors

Sector	Inflow state capital (US$ and percentage of total)
Manufacturing	414 (23.9%)
Wholesale and retail trade	375 (21.6%)
Financial and insurance activities	233 (13.4%)
Electricity and gas	213 (12.3%)
Transportation and storage	132 (7.6%)
Mining and quarrying	148 (6.6%)
Information and communication	88 (5.1%)
Professional, scientific and technical activities	63 (3.6%)
Administrative and support service activities	37 (2.2%)
Construction	25 (1.5%)

Table 6.2 The top-seven clusters (following the analysis in Babic (2021)) in terms of strategic investment (control-to-portfolio ratio) and (in)equality of invested amounts (Gini coefficient)

Cluster	Control–portfolio ratio	Gini coefficient
Western European manufacturing	1.02	0.63
Western European transportation and storage	8.4	0.7
Western European electricity and gas	69.2	0.64
North American mining and quarrying	2.03	0.79
Northern European transportation and storage	17.9	0.62
Southern European electricity and gas	18.7	0.82
Southern European manufacturing	28.9	0.77

Note: See Table 3.5 for an explanation of both measures.

concentration. Table 6.1 gives an overview over the sectoral composition of foreign state investment, while Table 3.5 did the same for global macro-regions. Table 6.2 combines both and lists some of the most concentrated clusters in terms of overall investment and the comparability of investment stakes.

Many prominent cases of foreign state-led investment, like Gazprom (western European electricity and gas), the China National Offshore Oil Corporation (North American mining and quarrying) and Syngenta (western European manufacturing), are located within these clusters. Some clusters, like northern European transportation and storage, are thereby highly competitive: Dutch, German and French transportation firms are invested in British railway operations, and global logistic players like Dubai's DP World took over ports and ferries in the UK that represent focal nodes of the global logistical infrastructure. For other clusters, we already have anecdotal evidence that geoeconomic competition could play a role, for example the southern European electricity and gas cluster, where a recent takeover attempt of Portuguese utility provider EDP by China's state-owned Three Gorges failed spectacularly (Babic 2021).

Although this approach allows us to "see" where state capital is concentrated cross-border, it is not enough to determine real geoeconomic competition. What this shows is that there is at least a high concentration of comparably powerful states as owners that are invested in similar industrial targets in the same geographical area. Overall, three global industries stand out: manufacturing, energy production and distribution, and transportation and logistics. All three are important sectors for global economic development, and in all three areas we can expect geoeconomic dynamics arising in the next decade. From this starting point, it is possible to analyse in more depth and in more qualitative ways whether and how this concentration of state capital not only presents the potential for competition and conflict, but whether there are tangible dynamics already taking place. Such a global mapping approach to foreign state investment is important in the medium run: it can show us where potential competition and conflict in the global political economy are likely to happen in the next decade. In accordance with the theoretical considerations laid out in this chapter, such an empirical approach allows us to see and map potential hotspots of geoeconomic competition in the 2020s.

From integration to weaponization? Cases of geoeconomic competition

In order to illustrate this approach and make the phenomenon of geoeconomic competition more tangible, here I describe three cases which emerge from the analysis of the state ownership dataset employed in this book. All three are examples of what a research programme covering the 2020s could look like, with much more substantial research and embedding in existing larger conflicts around geoeconomic supremacy in the twenty-first century. They also follow the logic of state capital concentration described above in manufacturing (case 1), energy (case 2) and logistics and transportation (case 3).

Case 1: Chinese state-led investment in western European manufacturing

Since the early 2010s, Chinese outwards investment has been aimed at acquiring technological and industrial know-how as well as assets, especially in Europe (Meunier 2014). Since 2015, this buying up of key technological firms has accelerated with the announcement of the comprehensive MiC industrial strategy. The years 2015 and 2016 saw record inflows of Chinese investment into western Europe, with the profile of takeovers closely matching the ten designated MiC key sectors (Jungbluth 2018). This obvious targeting of world-leading western European technology firms comes back in the analysed western European manufacturing cluster, with firms like Syngenta, KraussMaffei and FACC being acquired. The political backlash to this strong concentration of Chinese investment into western Europe came quickly, with countries like Germany and France amending foreign trade laws to block this type of investment (Stompfe 2020). Germany even employed extraordinary state powers to avert the planned investment of Chinese state-owned State Grid Corporation of China (SGCC) into German network grid provider 50Hertz in 2018. Since the existing foreign trade law was not applicable here, the German government, under the leadership of the economics ministry, used its state-owned development bank, Kreditanstalt für Wiederaufbau, to acquire the stake before SGCC could do so. This unprecedented tactical move produced heated debates on the role of the state in the German economy (Babic & Dixon 2022). Shortly afterwards, the EU itself introduced comprehensive foreign investment screening mechanisms as an answer to Chinese takeovers. Geoeconomic competition from Chinese state-led investment thus urged European policy-making to gradually reverse its "global level playing field" approach to global investment and introduce protectionist measures. This emerging conflict between Chinese firms, European targets and European host states, as well as the EU, is a prime example of state-led geoeconomic competition.

Case 2: Russian state-led investment in western European electricity and gas

Russian state-led investment has always been a major factor in western Europe's energy mix, thereby representing the largest export market for Russian gas and oil. Up until the late 2000s, this mutual dependency of both Russia and western Europe did not cause major political issues. However, rising geopolitical tensions in two "gas wars" in 2006 and 2009, as well as a two real wars with Ukraine in the form of Russian invasions in 2014 and 2022, changed the picture. Russian state-led investment through its state-owned firms like Gazprom has thereby played a major role in shaping these conflicts. The increasingly aggressive expansion into western European markets, especially after the successive liberalization of the European energy market, also included major investments in companies such as Germany-based Wingas. Projects like Nord Stream 2, which were mainly carried out by state-owned vehicles, have been increasing this geoeconomic competition for European gas and oil market shares, and raised the geopolitical stakes for Russia until the cancellation of the project by Germany in 2022. Within these markets, Gazprom competes with other large state-owned energy giants like Vattenfall for market share. Next to the Western sanctions regime, which so far has only indirectly targeted Gazprom, future geoeconomic competition between such firms is likely to be affected by global decarbonization efforts: whereas states as owners like Russia are almost unwavering in their support for their fossil fuel industries and employ them as geopolitical weapons (see the analysis in Chapter 4), others like Vattenfall are embracing renewables in a bid to become market leaders in markets like offshore wind (Chowdhary 2021). The geoeconomic competition for one of the largest energy markets in Europe is a key example involving future energy transformation and strategic positioning within these dynamics by states as owners. These current and future conflicts do not only include a (politically divided) Europe as the host of this investment, but also crucially the state-owned energy firms competing for market shares and influence. In a latest show of force, Gazprom first withheld and then agreed to slightly increase gas supplies to Europe, which began to struggle with exploding gas prices in the autumn of 2021 (Shiryaevskaya & Mazneva 2021). This move served the Russian government well in the preparation for the war in Ukraine, in which European gas dependence is a key obstacle for stronger sanctions against Russia. Such tactical aspects are often interpreted as part of a longer-term geoeconomic strategy that aims at maintaining the crucial role Russian gas still plays for European energy security. Consequently, European powers retaliated against some of Russia's state-owned entities for their bolstering of Putin's invasion of Ukraine, but have not gone so far as cutting all ties in the light of the high degree of gas dependence of some EU member states. An additional geoeconomic aspect are third parties like the USA, who are producers of relatively cheap shale gas and have an external interest in replacing the Russian gas supply in Europe (Yergin 2020). The sanctions for Nord Stream 2 under the Trump administration and its later cancellation by Germany are a case in point that extend this conflict involving state-led investment forms at its core.

Case 3: German and French investment in northern European transportation and storage

Germany and France both have a legacy of state-owned "national champions", which dominated industrial policy-making in the second half of the twentieth century. The privatization waves of the late 1980s and 1990s transformed these national champions in different ways, as we saw in Chapter 4. Many large-scale energy and infrastructure providers were only partly privatized, or the state retained a so-called golden share with a veto right (as with, e.g., French Engie and German Telekom). Another group of national champions in the transportation sector, however, remained in the state's hands, such as transportation and logistics firms like GeoPost/La Poste (France) and Schenker/DB (Germany). By adapting internationalization strategies, these firms leveraged their strong domestic backgrounds as large-scale employers and investors to compete in global markets. The entrance into the northern European, and here specifically the UK, market is especially attractive for those logistic firms, because it combines a large, high-income consumer market with crucial international transportation nodes. In a world that is increasingly reliant on well-functioning transportation infrastructure, the capture of those nodes and networks by state-led investment is a major source of geoeconomic competition. Firms like GeoPost rely already on a vast network of logistical nodes for their operation, with over 840 international hubs in 23 countries (GeoPost 2018). Given that both France and Germany are EU members, this dynamic could also turn out to lead to increased cooperation instead of competition in global markets: plans for a new European industrial strategy and the creation of "European champions" could also affect the logistics and transportation business in order to build powerful state-owned multinationals in an increasingly important global logistics market.

These three examples illustrate potential and ongoing "hot" cases of state-led geoeconomic competition. To be precise, geoeconomic competition is not the only plausible consequence of foreign state investment in a geoeconomic world. There are at least two other possible modalities that play a role in contemporary international politics. One follows from competition, namely potential *conflict*. This situation arises when state-led investment leads to political backlashes either in the host country or among different investors competing for similar targets. The example of 50Hertz described above is a case in point. A third modality is *cooperation*, which can happen between two states as investors, the investing state and the host government, or the investing state and a private actor. Examples for such cooperation are the agreement between the Putin and Modi governments to push through a deal between Russian state-owned Rosneft and Indian Oil producer Essar despite political backlash in 2017 (see Chapter 4); and the emerging cooperation between Russian state-owned Rosatom and UAE-owned DP World on securing important logistic routes in the Arctic (Kolodyazhnyy *et al.* 2021). While all three modalities play a role in the current state investment landscape, how exactly each constellation develops needs to be determined on a case-by-case basis. In general, speaking of a more competitive and conflictive geoeconomic environment into which state capital moves is a useful way of describing the politics of foreign state investment for the next decade.

Global rivalries, but different this time

If my analysis of the coming geoeconomic decade is, at least in its broad lines, accurate, the question remains what this means for the future of the competing state and its possible demise. As I argue throughout this book, the rise of state capital is not so much a countermovement to neoliberal globalization, but rather neoliberalism's own creation. As such, it might very well be that the various maladies and the slow but final demise of neoliberal globalization also means writing the requiem for the competing state of the early twenty-first century. However, as Chapter 2 has demonstrated, different historical state forms *transform* rather than vanish entirely. The emergence of new state forms is closely tied to historical developments that either have an effect on state transformations or are themselves the product of these transformations. Either way, an entire replacement of the competing state is unlikely, given basic economic interdependencies and existing cross-border ties that will not disappear overnight.

One possible scenario of framing the future of the competing state could be the upcoming "new Cold War" between China and the USA. The fact that the various state-led geoeconomic dynamics involve more actors than those two superpowers does not mean that such a framing is entirely obsolete. From recent research into the emerging "infrastructure scramble" that accompanies the new Cold War, we know that many sites of competition and conflict are located outside of China and the USA, from Africa to Latin America and from Europe to Asia.[15] By mobilizing state power through investment, regulation, diplomacy and other foreign policy and economic tools, the USA and China aim to position themselves in a "geopolitical-economic competition to integrate value chains anchored by their domestic lead firms through the financing and construction of transnational infrastructure" (Schindler *et al.* 2021: 1). The geoeconomic aspects of this infrastructure scramble are clear: the new global rivalries are not fought out in a classical geopolitical security sense, but by competing for transnational infrastructures. This new territorial logic also produces new forms and instruments of geoeconomic competition, of which one is state-led investment.

If we follow this analysis of the new Cold War, the competing state would not come to an abrupt end, but rather be instrumentalized in the course of the coming decade. The *integration* of state capital into existing structures of globalized capitalism during the neoliberal period could enable its *weaponization* in a geoeconomic world. This is especially the case for competition-prone sectors like global infrastructures that Schindler and colleagues identify as a crucial battleground of the new Cold War. We have seen in the above analysis that, next to manufacturing and energy production and distribution, infrastructures for logistics and transport are sectors where global state capital is

---

15. See the important work from Schindler & Kanai (2021).

highly concentrated. The global competition for the control of these physical as well as digital infrastructures is hence a major hotspot defining world politics for the 2020s. The involvement of states via direct investment and ownership in these sectors is an important asset and calculus for geoeconomic strategies. As with Covid-19, the consequences of a possible weaponization of state capital for geoeconomic ends differ per competing state strategy. Those at the financial end of the spectrum will be less involved in strategic disputes than more controlling strategies.

With all this being said, it is important to note that the "new" Cold War will indeed be new. The rise of the USA–China global rivalry out of the rubble of neoliberal globalization is in many ways hard to compare to the USA–Soviet standoff of the twentieth century. One difference is the varying territorial logics (geopolitical versus transnational). Another important distinction is that the globalized economy of the twenty-first century represents a profoundly different agency space from the twentieth-century world economy that was still mostly organized according to national borders. Within this space, different instruments and strategies are being employed rather than a simple geopolitical projection of state power abroad. Instead, as we have seen, geoeconomic instruments and strategies prevail, from capturing important global assets to controlling value chains across multiple states and jurisdictions. This different international or transnational environment in which the new global rivalries are being conducted also becomes a potential and real source of instability. While the "old" Cold War at times only avoided nuclear catastrophe by sheer chance, it was for the most part a geopolitical standoff between two relatively stable blocks of nation states with fairly predictable behaviour. The strategies and effects of geoeconomic competition in the new Cold War are, however, much less predictable. State capital is exemplary of this, as it first almost seamlessly integrated into global markets and corporate networks, only to be potentially weaponized within a few years of global turbulence. What seemed like a "good bargain" a few years ago might turn out to be problematic for many hosts of state capital as geoeconomic calculations change the rules of the game. Another at least as important source of potential instability going forward into the next decades is the interplay between states as owners and climate change, which is analysed in the remainder of this chapter.

The long game: state capital and climate change

For many developed economies, serious climate change mitigation policies have for a long time only played a role in so far as they were promises for the future. Targets like limiting global warming to 1.5°C in the Paris climate accords appeared to be concrete and quantifiable, but often turned out to not be followed by concrete steps to reach this goal. In recent years, partly because of the evident increase in catastrophic climate events, governments around the world are being pressured by civil society actors to finally take climate change seriously as the single overarching threat to human life on earth. Global climate movements like Fridays for Future or Extinction Rebellion gave this urgency a platform and voice, demanding immediate political action. States see themselves as confronted with two countercurrent forces. On the one side, decarbonization and getting to a low-or zero-carbon economy is in the object-ive interest of any government worldwide. The calculation here is simple: only an emissions-free world can create stable natural circumstances, which are the necessary conditions for the continued existence of socially organized forms like states. On the other side, a mixture of the psychological denial of the existence of an *actual* climate crisis, the short-termism of many domestic and international political horizons, vested "carbon interests" and capitalist path dependencies (e.g. in industrial organization) introduce obstacles and postponements to objectively necessary climate action. In order to realize an emissions-free world, a fundamental socio-economic transformation that rec-onciles the objectively necessary with the practically doable is the *conditio sine qua non* of avoiding climate catastrophe.

Research into the possibilities and limitations of such a fundamental trans-formation introduced the idea of the *environmental state* (Duit *et al.* 2016; Eckersley 2020). This is "a state that possesses a significant set of institutions and practices dedicated to the management of the environment and societal–environmental interactions" (Duit *et al.* 2016: 5). This state form is sometimes referred to as a normative goal of government action towards "greening" the state, society and the economy (Eckersley 2004). In other cases, the environ-mental state is used as a descriptive category to benchmark the ongoing trans-formation of states into "green" ones (Sommerer & Lim 2016). In both cases, however, the overarching motive is to better understand and enable green tran-sitions by mobilizing statecraft. Within this discussion, scholars also impor-tantly scrutinize the limitations and boundaries of the environmental state from a critical perspective. Studies about the "glass ceiling" (Hausknost 2020) of environmental states, or the discursive instrumentalization of the concept (Hatzisavvidou 2020), add important perspectives on how to critically engage with the problematic aspects of the environmental state.

From a state capital perspective, three questions arise regarding the role of the state in a global green transition. First, how can we conceptually think about the role of the state as an owner within the environmental state discus-sion? Second, what is the role and extent of state capital in global carbon and fossil fuel investment? Third, what are the pathways to decarbonize the state as an owner and how do competing states differ in this respect? The remainder of this chapter addresses these three questions. Despite the urgency of a global green transition, this aspect of state investment is the most long term as it concerns the fate of the global political economy until at least the end of this century.

Thinking differently about the environmental state

Following Andreas Duit, the environmental state perspective deals most explicitly with issues like *regulating* other (mostly corporate) actors, for example through law-making; *redistributing* environmental harm, for example through taxes; *administrating* environmental protection, for example through environmental agencies; and *producing, supporting* and *distributing knowledge* about environmental change, for example through university research funding (Duit 2016). These four aspects are a quite comprehensive description of the various tasks of the environmental state in the twenty-first century. At the same time, each of those aspects fall under a *managerial* understanding of the environmental state. This means that the state is portrayed as the prime actor coordinating, managing and if necessary intervening in the ongoing transformation processes in society and the economy.

This managerial understanding is useful, as it allows us to see where states meet their obligations, for example regarding international agreements like the Paris goals. It also enables us to point out different areas where state action and regulation can go further and where civil society can press for more radical change. Finally, it also allows us to critique the potentials and limitations of state power in bringing about objectively necessary changes, as is already being done within the existing literature. From a state capital perspective, however, an important component is underrepresented in the discussions on the environmental state, namely the role of the state *as carbon owner itself*. While states do regulate other actors and manage socio-economic processes, they are in many cases themselves profiting from carbon-intensive business practices like fossil fuel extraction. In fact, today's global oil and gas production is dominated strongly by NOCs, and states are still responsible for about 40 per cent of global investment in the fossil fuel sector.[16] This is not much less than what NOCs produced and controlled almost a decade ago (Hults *et al.* 2012). This leads to a paradoxical situation: some of the very states that are supposed to manage the green transition are themselves carbon incumbents and profit from the

---

16. For recent studies on this topic see Alkadiri and Ewers (2020) and Manley and Heller (2021).

production, sale and investment of and in fossil fuels. A prime example of this problematic dichotomy is Norway. While the Norwegian SWF pledges to continuously divest from fossil fuel-producing firms, the Norwegian *government* continues to expand its licensing for fossil fuel exploration in the Arctic (Arvin 2021a). The revenues from this business model are then partly used to fund its climate-conscious SWF investment strategy.

Such examples illustrate why it is important to consider both the managerial as well as the ownership aspects of the environmental state. Existing studies on the environmental state, however, pay less attention to how states as owners behave, what their investment strategies are and what meaningful decarbonization steps would look like. A state capital perspective can shed light on these questions by asking what states do, not as market regulators but as market participants. The benefit of introducing such a perspective is also a practical one. Changing environmental laws and aiming to induce behavioural changes through regulations and incentives is often a long-winded, steep process jeopardized by partisan divides, legal setbacks and uncertain implementation. Flanking these necessary societal negotiations with quick and effective measures like the disinvestment of state carbon capital is an important but often neglected aspect of environmental state discussions.

Conceptually, we can draw again on Gramscian state theory in order to think through the ownership or investment side of the environmental state. As proponents of the environmental state also emphasize, states are not unitary agents, but rather "fragmented, self-contradictory, and only partly coherent" (Duit *et al.* 2016: 4). Gramscian state theory finds the reasons for this fragmentation in the various state apparatuses and the respective contradictory logics, interests and power relations inscribed into them (Jessop 2007; Poulantzas 1969). Far from being unitary actors, state apparatuses hence often develop lives of their own, which can thus push forward or restrain state transformation.[17] The vehicles and apparatuses that govern the state as an owner hence represent a specific aspect of the environmental state that needs to be analysed in different ways than its managerial counterparts. It is, for instance, relevant that SOE governance has, in most cases, a relative distance from other state apparatuses like environmental legislation. This is especially the case for transnational investment vehicles, which are often managed by professional elites and are not directly controlled by ministries, as they used to be in the twentieth century. Depending on the particular constellations of state and societal power

---

17. For state apparatuses pushing transformation see Block (2008); for blocking full transformation see Weiss (2003).

inscribed into these apparatuses, this distance is greater or smaller and so is the relative autonomy of different apparatuses.

I argue that in order to understand the ownership role of the environmental state beyond its managerial aspects, we need to focus on how carbon state capital behaves in the global political economy. To provide a first step into this direction, I first scrutinize what we mean when we say "carbon state capital", and then discuss the decarbonization potentials of different carbon state ownership strategies.

Oil, gas and other dirty assets: what is carbon state capital?

Speaking of carbon state capital necessitates a definition: if states are supposed to be carbon owners, what is "carbon" ownership exactly? One simple way of answering this is to look at fossil fuel industries exclusively. States that are directly invested in fossil fuels do not only receive profits from this investment, but often also directly control their invested firms. This gives them significant leverage over firm strategy, especially when it comes to decarbonization efforts. This approach is chosen by most studies on NOCs that aim to analyse the direct involvement of states into fossil fuel extraction and production. While fossil fuels represent the largest chunk of carbon state capital, they are not the only CO_2-intensive sector that is state-invested. Other industries like petrochemical production, pesticides and fertilizers, cement and steel production, air transport and mining are also relevant and represent investment targets for carbon state capital. In fact, each of those industries contributes a significant share to yearly total greenhouse gas emissions.[18] If we take these investments on board, we get a more comprehensive picture of states as global carbon owners and investors.

Such a state capital perspective consequently takes not only particular vehicles (like NOCs) and their specific ties (into gas, oil and coal) seriously, but the state as an owner. This makes it possible to map the "real" carbon footprint of the environmental state by incorporating not only the investment ties of specific vehicles into specific industries, but of state ownership itself. This allows us also to critically scrutinize claims by states and state-owned investment vehicles of carbon "divestment", especially when this type of divestment concerns only direct oil and gas exploration and production, but often not downstream businesses and other related industries like petrochemicals.

---

18. See, for instance, for cement Fennell *et al.* (2021); for steel Fan and Friedmann (2021); and for the (petro)chemical industry Levi and Cullen (2018).

If we adopt such a state capital perspective, two questions emerge. First, what is the relation of the carbon footprint of cross-border state investment compared to domestic investment? Second, what is the scope of industries we should take into account to understand the carbon footprint of competing states? Both questions are relevant for understanding what state carbon capital is, and what the decarbonization potential of states as global carbon owners can be.

Regarding the first question, a comparison of the domestic and transnational volumes of carbon state investment shows that for most large owners the transnational dimension is less significant. As an estimate,[19] direct ownership of carbon capital is, for owners like China, around less than 1 per cent of its total investment, while for the UAE or Russia it is below 3 per cent. While these numbers are fairly low, we need to take into account two caveats. The first is that the sample used here pertains only to the direct state ownership of carbon-producing firms and excludes subsidiaries that are not directly state owned. This automatically reduces the number of transnationally held carbon capital. Second, most carbon capital is naturally domestically owned, as large utility firms responsible for energy security have a long history of state ownership. The share of the competing state on national energy production is hence almost by definition lower.

However, despite its lower total share, transnationally owned carbon capital also contains a decarbonization advantage. States that own carbon capital outside their borders usually do not hold this for reasons of domestic energy security. Rather, they exploit the opportunities offered to them by the transnational agency space. This might in some cases – like the Gulf states – be a vital component for a competing state's "business model". It is, however, easier to divest from cross-border carbon assets and investments than to give up domestic energy security that is tied to fossil fuels in the most cases. On top of this, there are some competing states that indeed own a quite large share of their total carbon investment cross-border. Most prominent among them is Norway, which is estimated to own around three-quarters of its total carbon investment transnationally. Others like Singapore, Canada or Sweden also invest significant amounts of state carbon capital outside their own borders. This aspect increases the decarbonization potentials of some competing states compared to others that hold most of their carbon assets in domestic energy generation or other vital industries.

19. I use Bureau van Dijk's ORBIS database to estimate these numbers. The sample I use is from August 2021 and entails only directly owned carbon firms. This is slightly different from the dataset used to analyse the general state capital distribution in Chapter 3.

This leads us also to the second question regarding the scope of industries that should be taken into account when we speak of "carbon" state capital. A first criterion should be, as I argued above, a broadening of our understanding of this phenomenon beyond the direct extraction and production of fossil fuels. Related industries like cement production, petrochemicals or fertilizers are also carbon emitting and state ownership plays a significant role here. Second, we should introduce a caveat and not regard state ownership in industries like food production or infrastructure development as "carbon" state capital per the definition. Despite their significance for global emissions, food production and other vital industries should maybe even become *more* state-owned in an age of increasing climate change-induced food insecurity and global coordination and distribution problems. The strategy here would not be to seek to divest from these vital industries, but rather to transform them into green industries under public control. Third, and related to the first two points, we should take into account industries and sectors where decarbonization is straightforward and feasible from a state capital perspective. Not all sectors are as clearly and straightforwardly problematic as large national oil and gas producers. Take mobility and transportation as an example: while state ownership in airlines can be regarded as a sector which should be taken into account for decarbonizing state capital, national transportation and railway systems are less clear-cut. The transportation of vital goods like food and medicine are still dependent on fossil fuelled means like motorized trucks in most countries. Decarbonizing these sectors is difficult, not least because state capital is often interwoven with private investment, for example when states own roads and railways but the operators are private companies (see Liu & Dixon 2021). For an effective and rapid carbon state capital decarbonization and divestment, the more clear-cut cases of carbon state ownership should have priority.

By taking these differentiations seriously, I argue that we can develop a comprehensive and concrete approach to the decarbonization of states as owners. Such an approach echoes the recent call by Robyn Eckersley for a renewed critical strategy at decarbonization efforts which she describes as "critical problem-solving" (Eckersley 2020). Drawing on a critical Gramscian perspective enables us to disentangle the various aspects of the state as a carbon owner, while the (pragmatic) push for feasible and rapid transitions brings an important problem-solving angle to the issue at hand. This fusion of critical inquiry and pragmatic problem-solving aspects leads to the two differentiations made above. In sum, we need to distinguish competing state ownership from energy security and other domestically oriented ownership and acknowledge different decarbonization potentials in both spheres. In addition, we should be aware of the fact that "carbonized" industries are not all the same when it comes to state investment: there is more than fossil fuel ownership where states are involved in carbon-emitting industries; some industries and sectors are more vital for the functioning of economies and societies than others and should hence be treated differently; and some are more straightforward to disentangle and decarbonize than others.

With these provisions, I seek to add another crucial layer to the developed state capital perspective. So far, I have covered some of the general aspects that a state capital perspective can contribute to the study of environmental states and decarbonization potentials. However, one key topic of this book is the distinction between the ideal types of financial and controlling state strategies. This strategic distinction can add an important factor to the more general discussions of what state capital can and cannot achieve within the global energy transition.

Carbonized strategies

When referring to "decarbonization" in general, I mean the process of "getting rid" or eliminating a CO_2-producing asset (or the emitting parts of this asset). This can principally work in two ways: either the asset owner decides to redirect the investment in a carbon asset towards alternative, sustainable assets (divesting); or the owner lets the asset "strand", meaning that the owner stops producing or exploiting the CO_2-emitting asset altogether. The first point does not mean that there will be an effective reduction of emissions, as other buyers can simply continue exploiting the sold asset (see, e.g., Christophers 2021). However, if states as the largest producers of fossil fuels decide to eliminate massive carbon assets from their ownership portfolio, they undoubtedly signal to global markets that CO_2-intensive assets will eventually be stranded and hence do not represent a viable long-term investment goal (Baron & Fischer 2015). A third option is to "green" the CO_2-emitting aspects of an asset, which is more a socio-technical question of making production processes and the like emissions-free. For states as owners, the first two options will be the most immediately relevant ones, and they reflect the different investment profiles (portfolio and majority) discussed below.

Decarbonizing states as owners requires us not only to think about the general aspects of carbon state capital, but also about the different decarbonization potentials of competing states. On the most basic level, this concerns the ability to rapidly divest from fossil fuels without running into either a devastating economic crisis or even bringing about serious political instability by this fast transformation. This dependence on *state* ownership of fossil fuels for economic and political stability, however, mainly concerns a group of states where political and economic power are intimately tied to the state (elite) control of the extraction, production and sale of fossil fuels like in many of today's monarchies in the Gulf region. Large owners like Saudi Arabia or Kuwait have almost all (the former) or close to 90 per cent (the latter) of their carbon state capital invested in majority stakes. For most of the other competing states, the abandoning of carbon investment, beyond fossil fuels, will not lead to major crises, but will rather require a strategic reorientation of its investment. This is where a differentiation between more financialized and more controlling strategies becomes a useful guiding principle.

From a financialized strategy perspective, carbon investment is one among many asset classes that states as owners are involved in. Given the nature of these financial strategies, carbon capital is here on average invested via portfolio stakes. This means that states usually own small parts of firms that are counted as carbon intensive, for instance carbon multinationals like Shell or BP; or they are invested in global industrial emitters like cement or steel firms. The relevant point here is that most of this investment is usually not conducted because these are CO_2-intensive companies. States as the owners of vehicles with portfolios invested in carbonized assets usually do this as a means of gaining a return on investment. *Where* this return on investment is being realized is most often a question of profits rather than of sector or industry. In other words, it is the profitability of these CO_2-intensive industries that decides about whether state capital is allocated there.[20] With, for instance, rising carbon taxes or other regulatory moves that reduce the profitability of these sectors, an outflow of state capital is to be expected for most financial competing state strategies.

This circumstance is especially pertinent for owners with vehicles that "mimic" other private institutional investors, for example by closely aligning their investment strategy with well-known indices. Among the top clients of index provider firms like MSCI are state-owned vehicles like SWFs.[21] By allocating a certain amount of their equity investment into the hands of major index providers, state-owned vehicles become partially passive surfers on global market dynamics. Although most SWFs still exert enough discretionary action when it comes to replicating indices, they in sum broadly follow global market trends.[22] A future dwindling profitability and the lower market capitalization of carbon firms is hence likely to lead to disinvestment and to a shift of those funds into alternative assets. This almost "automatic" aspect of

---

20. Existing studies on the "political" aspects of, for example, SWF investment remain inconclusive about whether portfolio investment really has a political steering aspect; see, for example, Amar *et al.* (2018) and Johan *et al.* (2013).

21. See Wigglesworth (2020) as well as the self-description of MSCI regarding their main asset owner clients on their website: https://www.msci.com/our-clients/asset-owners.

22. See Petry *et al.* (2021: 162) for the relationship between SWFs and investment indices.

global financial investment dynamics also influences the investment decisions of states as owners with large pools of portfolio investment. In sum, the relative liquidity of portfolio investment increases the decarbonization potentials of this strategic profile drastically.

On the other side, more controlling strategies do not display similar levels of liquidity and flexibility. Competing states with a controlling strategy usually invest their capital in majority stakes of cross-border-owned firms. This means that on average they hold large and quite inflexible positions in these firms, which are often also direct subsidiaries of domestic SOEs. To divest from these assets would hence mean giving up on either large and expensive acquisitions or reducing the number of subsidiaries cross-border. This is a fundamentally different situation from that of financialized strategies: as I have argued, controlling strategies are often motivated by cross-border asset capture, the acquisition of specific know-how or the control of vital nodes of global value chains and infrastructures. This type of investment often targets particular firms and industries that help in realizing those goals. This means that it is not primarily the *profitability* of these investments that drives cross-border investment, but specific types of assets and industries. Consequently, controlling strategies are much less flexible in simply switching from carbon-intensive to low-carbon investment alternatives. Many of the controlling strategies even aim at controlling cross-border carbon capital, as is the case for the Russian or Gulf states' strategies.

This lower flexibility and liquidity are thus potentially bad news for divestment and decarbonization efforts. Controlling strategies are from a theoretical standpoint much less likely to engage in rapid decarbonization if their investment strategy is not solely motivated by pure profitability aspects. In the worst case scenario, controlling strategies could even suffer disproportionally from falling profitability and shrinking market valuation of carbon assets in the future. Since these competing states are more or less "stuck" with their cross-border invested carbon capital, many of those investments could turn into so-called stranded assets. This asset type is broadly defined as an investment which is expected to stop returning a profit before the end of its life cycle. Stranded assets are thus leading to economic losses (see Caldecott 2017: 2). In the case of controlling strategies, these losses can amount to large sums. If states hold on to average majority positions in their (carbon) assets cross-border, the cumulative effect of a stranding in the future will be felt much more strongly than for financial strategies. Owners like Russia, India and Myanmar will have to rethink their strategic exposure to this issue. For another group of small countries where state carbon ownership makes up a significant share of their GDP (or total state assets), like Azerbaijan or Kuwait, these problems will be even more virulent in the coming years.

Decarbonizing through disinvestment? Towards concrete strategies

The debates about the potentials and "glass ceilings" of the environmental state show that it is necessary to flank these general discussions with a more granular look at different aspects of how the state relates to environmental degradation. Through a Gramscian state-theoretic lens, it is possible to focus on state ownership and state investment as being controlled by specific state apparatuses that are not always visible in more abstract discussions. The analysis above shows that such a perspective enables us to ask concrete questions that are crucial both for the future of competing states but also for the mitigation potential of environmental states: what is state carbon capital? How should we understand its transnational aspects? How does the divestment from carbonized state capital relate to economic and political stability? And which strategies are more or less likely to succeed with which possible reverberations? It is this series of analytical distinctions between various owners, strategies and decarbonization potentials that is crucial to building a good understanding of carbon state capital going forward.

As a bottom line, I argue that it is indeed possible to sketch ideal-typical decarbonization strategies for states as owners. These strategies then have to be implemented concretely on the ground and aligned with different local circumstances. This means that the above-mentioned catalogue of questions about industrial specificity, extent of transnational carbon investment, political stability, varying investment strategies and other issues can be put to work in case studies. Climate change and its mitigation attempts will be the single most existential political issue for the next decades, and the role of the state in these mitigation efforts is becoming more virulent again. Beyond the important general groundwork conducted in the environmental state literature, we also need to be able to grasp the socio-economic foundations and variation of carbon state investment as one major obstacle and potential for greening the state.

With these analytical provisions, the crucial question for the competing state is which role it will play in a "green" global political economy of the future. Two broad alternatives are thinkable: either competing states divest from their carbonized capital and reinvest this capital elsewhere (probably for financial strategies) or they withdraw, and in the worst case amortize this capital in the long run (probably for controlling strategies). Or these competing states find a way of decarbonizing large parts of their carbon investment without necessarily having to divest. While this scenario also depends on the type of investment – oil assets are harder to "decarbonize" than investment in transportation and logistics – it also involves the existence (or lack) of a long-term strategic vision. As we saw in Chapter 4, heavily carbonized owners like Russia and Saudi Arabia can have quite different views on the long-term viability of fossil fuel and carbon investment. While the latter is already engaging in long-term diversification of its investment, in order to avoid having to deal with a large amount of stranded assets among other things, the former seems to be more engaged in tactical rather than strategic thinking so far (Bradshaw *et al.* 2019). For competing state elites that do not engage in this sort of strategic thinking, decarbonization could happen involuntarily through global market shifts and stranded assets. Whether states as owners pick one of the other strategies of (conscious) divestment or decarbonization will also be determined by the various analytical questions formulated and explained in this section.

7

Conclusion: states, markets and the future of globalization

In Chapter 1, I described this book as a challenge to the standard narrative of the rise of state capitalism in the last two decades. The key argument I developed is that it is not an abstract statism that rises in the global political economy, but specific forms of *transnational state capital*. To substantiate this argument, I drew on a set of different techniques such as a historical account of the rise and fall of state intervention (Chapter 2), large-scale, firm-level data analysis (Chapter 3), in-depth case studies (Chapters 4 and 5) and a policy-oriented embedding of these arguments in current debates (Chapter 6). As the preceding chapters demonstrate, cross-border-owned state capital and state-led investment are phenomena that are often more nuanced and harder to grasp than categorical thinking like "states against markets" suggests. *States can also be global market actors.* Through exploring historical, conceptual, quantitative, qualitative and policy-oriented aspects of the renewed involvement of states into global markets, I illustrated one novel aspect of this fact. A main takeaway of this study is that a strong empirical focus is needed to develop a better understanding of how and to what extent states become market actors, and what this means for different aspects of international politics. This contribution can hopefully inform some of the more abstract discussions on the merits and limits of catch-all concepts like state capitalism.

This empirical focus is, however, not taking place in a vacuum, but is guided by conceptual considerations. I introduced two main concepts that aid the analysis of this book: the transnational agency space and the competing state. Both concepts are connected to previous work on the unevenness of socio-economic spaces in the global political economy and on state transformations that brought about different state forms over recent decades. It is important to keep in mind that these concepts are not primarily theoretical contributions, but conceptual tools to better understand how states as owners gain agency, and how this agency translates into (partial) state transformation. The transnational agency space concept is not a full-fledged theory of spatial dynamics within global capitalism. Rather, it is an instrument to understand what enabled state capital to rise during neoliberal globalization, given that it could not do so before. It is the existence of global trade and investment regimes, of open equity markets, of financial institutions allowing for financing and leveraging, of frameworks for investment protection and non-discrimination, or the offshorization and transnationalization of financial services and professionals that enabled the rise of state capital in the global economy. Taken together, this creates an opportunity space for states to thrive as owners. Furthermore, the concept of the competing state does not correspond to a new theory of the (capitalist) state. Rather, the competing state concept is the further development of theories of the competition state that emphasized the "defensive" adaptation mechanisms of nation states vis-à-vis globalization. The competing state concept captures a different, more "offensive" aspect of this engagement with globalization. Instead of the domestic reconfiguration of labour markets and welfare systems to attract capital, the competing state exploits previously unavailable opportunities for either asset capture or financial profits. Both concepts introduced in this book hence inform the empirical analysis and also contribute important building blocks for further discussions as laid out in the second part of this conclusion.

At different points in this study, I maintained the stance that the role states play as global owners in today's global economy is unprecedented. This might sound like an exaggeration, as we know of massive state-corporate hybrids such as the Dutch or English East India companies going as far back as the sixteenth century (Phillips & Sharman 2020). These company-states were in all likelihood more powerful amalgams of state and corporate power than today's states as owners are. Similarly, late nineteenth-century conglomerates and cartels, often state-owned in cases like France or Germany, also shaped international politics decisively. Notwithstanding these historical precedents, Chapter 2 argued that the emergence of states as global owners displays a *qualitative* difference to previous rounds of statist rearticulation. The integration of states as producers and owners in cross-border value chains and global production and investment networks displays a complexity that is new in the global economy (Oatley 2019). Large state-owned conglomerates and company-states certainly wielded more nominal power in international relations than SOEs do today. However, these actors were part of a world economy that was not defined by the deep and complex interdependence of today's globalized economy (Farrell & Newman 2019). This difference matters, especially for the question of how states and markets interact. In a world of complex interdependence, the lines between what states and what market actors do are much more blurred and more difficult to separate analytically. In fact, it could even be argued that today's large multinational companies, thus also transnational SOEs, are hardly unitary actors any more, but represent permeable networks holding together different functional units (see, e.g., Reurink & Garcia-Bernardo 2020). This has consequences for how states and corporations wield power in the global system: not through simply projecting power abroad, but through the integration into and exploitation of global networks. It is in this sense that I emphasize the "unprecedented" nature of the rise of states as global owners, and the consequences this integration has for our understanding of what states and markets are.

In the remainder of this conclusion, I outline two contributions of this book to current discussions on where states and markets are headed in the crisis of neoliberal globalization. The first contribution concerns the manifold debates on whether neoliberal globalization is in decay, and what role the rearticulation of statism in this context means. Based on the arguments developed in this book, I argue that such discussions are useful but often lack empirical nuance. The rise of state capital during neoliberal globalization illustrates how such discussions could profit from a better empirical basis that would also inform conceptual and theoretical statements. The second contribution relates to discussions on state transformations in the twenty-first century, and how a state capital perspective can add important arguments to these debates. State-led investment vehicles do play a role in the literature on state transformations, but are often subsumed under a governance-oriented framework. I argue that the state transformations following from the emergence of state capital are a distinct category, and that the related rise of the competing state is not trivial: if we want to understand the possibilities and limits of state capacity in the 2020s onwards, we need to integrate states as owners as a central cornerstone of this discussion. In the last part of this conclusion, I propose avenues for further research and include a section for how policy-makers can utilize the insights of this book for practical matters.

Between a rock and a hard place: the slow death of neoliberal globalization and supposed birth of neostatism revisited

Many announcements of the death of neoliberalism were premature as has been argued by different authors (see, e.g., Crouch 2011; Mirowski 2014). One of the problems that riddles the discussions on whether we are in a phase after neoliberalism is conceptual confusion. What is it that we actually want to express by referring to neoliberalism? Recent scholarship clarified many of the ambiguities and confusions of earlier discussions (Davies & Gane 2021; Hendrikse 2018; Huijzer 2021; Slobodian 2018). Here, I want to focus on a specific historical phase of the global political economy, which I refer to as neoliberal globalization (Scholte 2005). This concept is not another variety of the overall concept of neoliberalism, but describes a particular constellation of social forces and "social purpose" of the global order that shaped the last four decades. Following John Ruggie, international regimes consist of broadly two aspects: form and content (Ruggie 1982: 382). The former relates to the question of who holds power in the international system and hence determines whether an order is unipolar, multipolar or something else. The latter describes the specific purpose an order is supposed to fulfil. This social purpose is reflected in characterizations of global economic orders as "Keynesian" or "neoliberal". Accordingly, the postwar international order of embedded liberalism combined welfare-increasing liberal trade relations with the expansion of domestic welfare and social security in Europe, the USA and Japan. The following phase of neoliberal globalization rolled back many of those domestic social achievements by moving economic policy-making further away from democratic influence and "encasing" it, often at the supranational level (Slobodian 2018). Concretely, this process entailed the reconstitution and liberalization of global financial markets (Helleiner 1994), the deregulation of goods, service and labour markets (Peters 2008), the rollback or restructuring of social welfare systems towards greater flexibility and efficiency (Karimi 2016, ch. 6; Kus 2006) and attempts to increase "national competitiveness", for example through corporate tax competition in many OECD countries (Heimberger 2021).

With a more concrete understanding of what "neoliberal globalization" means it is also more feasible to judge whether this phase of organizing the global political economy is ending or not. In ongoing discussions, neoliberal globalization is sometimes described as being under strain, whereas others already identify the emergence of post-neoliberal political forms and regimes (Geva 2021). In an important contribution, Gerbaudo sees neoliberal globalization at an end and identifies a clear "ideological shift" towards "neostatism" (Gerbaudo 2021: 3). His book describes a framework that is reminiscent of Polanyi's pendulum as discussed in Chapter 6. In fact, the metaphor of a "great recoil" even uses Polanyian ideas to describe a statist "counterthrust" to neoliberal globalization (*ibid.*: 7). Gerbaudo's is the most clear-cut recent argument for a new statist epoch that will shape the 2020s. He explicitly frames neostatism as the ideological force that is ordering post-pandemic politics along left ("social protectionism") or right ("proprietarian protectionism") radical lines. This new statism represents a new *endopolitics* replacing neoliberalism's *exopolitics*. Instead of an ever-tighter growing together of the global economy based on cross-border and other "external" forms of integration, the neostatist endopolitics would lead to a stronger reshoring of global value chains and a re-embedding of societies and economies. Neoliberal globalization, put simply, would in such a post-neoliberal world be replaced by the triad of "sovereignty, protection and control" (*ibid.*: 205).

How does this analysis square with the rise of the competing state? In some ways, the reassertion of sovereignty and control could bring back state power over economic processes. Instead of desperately trying to recapture tax revenues, jobs and value chains through supply-side adjustments, neostatist politics would instead aim to "reinternalise capital, to re-embed economic processes in social and political institutions and to reaffirm a sense of interiority" (Gerbaudo 2021: 67). However, as this book has argued and demonstrated, the competing state of the twenty-first century is all but a domestically oriented state form. It draws its power to accumulate economic capital or assets under state control from the very fact that a globalized economy outside its own borders exists. The "exopolitics" of neoliberal globalization is the condition that allowed states like China or Norway to become large-scale global owners and move markets with their investment decisions. As I argued in Chapters 2 and 3, without the existence of a transnational agency space created by neoliberal globalization, the emergence of competing states would be technically impossible. Instead of reasserting state power, a "reinternalization" of capital accumulation as Gerbaudo envisages would for many states as large global owners mean an effective loss of structural power in important markets and sectors. Neostatism would consequently *not* be an attractive prospect for governments that are heavily invested in an open global economy.

Different from thinking in terms of states and markets as antagonistic forces, the analysis conducted in this book argues that many states could only expand their relative power in international politics once globalized markets opened up for them to accrue profits and assets. This argument is explicitly not building on the idea that "states" or economies as such somehow abstractly profited from globalized markets and liberalized trade relations, as a standard liberal argument would go. It is rather specific groups and particular interest coalitions within states that gain disproportionally from globalization and liberalization, while others lose out. What I argue here concerns specifically *states as economic owners* gaining from globalization. The fact that we saw a massive reconcentration of capital in state hands just a few years after the privatization waves of the 1990s is not a coincidence. It stems from the realization of governments that "state financialization" (Schwan *et al.* 2020) or the state becoming a global shareholder and owner (Wang 2015; Babic *et al.* 2020) opens up previously unavailable channels of wielding economic power. Different from competition state politics – which might square better with the argument of a relative loss of state power in the face of globalization – competing state politics are not signalling the ceding of power from "the state" towards "the market": rather the opposite, as I have argued throughout this book.

The type of power amassed over the years by states as owners is certainly not a "classical" site of state power, such as regulatory, legislative or executive power. Becoming global owners means for states first of all to enter the realm of markets. This also involves playing by the rules of global markets to a certain degree. However, as we saw in Chapter 6, the consequences that states as owners create for international politics are not trivial. States moving into global markets might not necessarily be the projection of state power into the economic realm that was feared by many observers over the last decade (see e.g. Bremmer 2010; Kurlantzick 2016). It nevertheless makes a difference whether states or private market actors are invested in corporations around the world. This is especially the case for those states as owners that embrace a long list of investment strategies that involve the acquisition and capturing of specific assets and know-how. Such geoeconomic strategies illustrate one important form of power states gain as global owners. They become able to acquire previously unreachable technologies, assets and knowledge which can be used to propel domestic development or increase domestic competitiveness (see, e.g., Hannas & Tatlow 2020). Another type of power states gain through global investment can be a relative strong position in certain markets and sectors, where their investment decisions (e.g. by states with financialized strategies) can move markets (see, e.g., Arvin 2021b).

These possibilities and increased structural power positions of states as owners were unthinkable in times when globalization and cross-border economic integration were not dominating factors in the global economy. To understand the demise of neoliberal globalization as a potential game-changer for increasing state power vis-à-vis markets would hence, at least in the sense described above, be a misleading conclusion. The example of state capital is an instructive one for discussions about the possible nature of a neostatist phase following after neoliberal globalization, and beyond the particular focus on states as owners. Analyses like Gerbaudo's (2021) highlight the "recoiling" character of neostatism and emphasize its diametric opposition to neoliberal globalization. In this perspective, state power is mainly thought of in opposition to markets, not *through* them. The example of state capital introduces necessary nuance to this argument. States do not necessary wield power *against* markets. On the contrary, through the increased access to global markets many states augmented their economic and structural power in the global political economy. This relation is of course also true when turned around. Market actors receive legal and political protection from states; they are being enabled to conduct business and generate profits within the frameworks states as regulatory forces provide. State and corporate power are not mutually exclusive categories.

The assumption of a neostatist phase is reminiscent of the rise of the protective state after the Second World War (see Chapter 2). Such a Polanyian "swinging back" to forms of state protection is, however, also unlikely in spheres beyond state capital. The existence of cross-border economic ties, value chains and global production networks is not just a number of different metaphors for neoliberal globalization. These forms of interdependence reflect a fundamental shift in how global production and exchange are organized today in comparison to earlier phases of global economic integration. The *systemic* character of the global economy that results from decades of neoliberal globalization (Oatley 2019; Robinson 2004) makes it difficult to roll it back simply by reclaiming protective state powers or pursuing "endopolitics". We can see this in the discussion around a possible deglobalization that some observers expect as a consequence of the recent Covid-19 crisis. Such a development can in fact be better described as "slowbalization", meaning the slowing of economic integration rather than a building back of existing economic ties and networks (Linsi 2021). However, even if the process of globalization ground to a halt it would not equate to deglobalization. As argued in Chapter 6, the existence of cross-border economic ties built during neoliberal globalization is rather being weaponized by powerful states and corporations than built back (see also Farrell & Newman 2019). The very existence of these ties grants some actors structural power positions which they would not have in a world without these channels of possible power projection.

To conclude, the example of state capital, which emerged during neoliberal globalization and which thrives on the investment opportunities created by neoliberalism's "exopolitics", shows how the future of globalization might be more nuanced than the strict opposition of states and markets and possible recoils suggests. Such nuance is not only warranted for theoretical reasons but for policy-making in times of crisis and transition. Rebalancing the relationship between states and markets will not mean the same in a world that is shaped by transnational economic relations and interdependencies. What "state" and "market" mean today is different from what they meant in the state transformations of the twentieth century. Acknowledging this could help in better dealing with economic interdependencies in the turbulent geoeconomic decades ahead of us.

Beyond governance: state capital and state transformations

The second debate to which the findings of this book can contribute important insights is the discussion on state transformations in the twenty-first century. I touched upon some of the details of how different historical state forms rose and fell in Chapter 2. Similarly, the description of the evolution of the competing state from the competition state of the 1990s suggests a phase of state transformation that is significant. Within the existing literature, state transformations are broadly understood as "fundamental changes of the state" (Huber *et al.* 2015: 1). These can involve various levels, dimensions and causes, as an impressive amount of case studies and analyses on the matter illustrates (see Leibfried *et al.* 2015 for an overview). Here, I put an emphasis on how the emergence of the competing state both transforms and is transformed by global and domestic forces and argue that this type of state transformation is typically overlooked in existing debates on the matter.

The competing state is a state form that draws both its legitimacy as well as its development potential from a globalized economy. This international or transnational aspect of the competing state is key to understand how the competition state of the heyday of neoliberal globalization was transformed – or at least significantly modified – in the last two decades. Given multiplying possibilities of investing surplus revenues in global markets in the 1990s and 2000s, states with such surpluses (from various sources) set up investment vehicles ranging from SWFs to SOEs and development banks to "reach out" and establish economic ties with the rest of the world. The fact that state-owned vehicles transnationalize and interact with global markets can be captured by existing conceptual notions such as "state internationalization". Within the more mainstream literature, however, such internationalization is often understood as the international extension or transformation of the sovereignty and authority of states (Zürn & Deitelhoff 2015). State capital, which is based on state ownership relations, is not a clear-cut case of the internationalization of *authority* per se. States do not reach out in a regulatory capacity, but do so rather as economic owners and market actors. Whereas the global environment hence influences state capital transnationalization, it does so in slightly different ways from a "classical" internationalization of authority alone.

On the domestic side, state capital transnationalization is also driven by particular constellations of social forces and structural constraints of political economies. As Huber *et al.* (2015) argue, the presence of "raw materials and human resources" (*ibid.*: 6) is a relevant domestic determinant of state transformations in general. This is especially true for the *competing* state. We have seen that only governments that can rely on a source of surplus funding are able to set up large-scale investment vehicles. This means that both the presence of natural or financial resources and the state capacity to turn these resources into state-led outwards investment are domestic conditions for the transformation into competing states. Different from the competition state, this aspect of the competing state is indeed *domestic*: it is not primarily the downwards pressure from neoliberal globalization that forces states to adapt domestically, but domestic aspects that bring about a change in investment behaviour. The aspect of domestic social forces championing these transformations is furthermore a decisive factor for understanding competing state transformations. As several studies have shown, state-led outward investment is often caused by elite contestation and consensus building in different political systems (see, e.g., Braunstein 2018; Clark & Monk 2010b; Schwartz 2012; Shih 2009). The transformation from competition into competing states is strongly driven by domestic elites seeking to reap the benefits of a globalized economy. It is however, again, *not* the case that states or state elites gain more governance-related autonomy through the transformations they push forward. This might seem paradoxical, as domestic political agency plays a much stronger role here than in most globalization-induced state transformations of the last decades. However, state elites do not mobilize resources solely to augment their "political" power, but to extend their global reach as economic owners. Both factors, namely increased domestic agency and the aims of this agency, are important contributions to the existing literature on state transformations and the recalibration of domestic and transnational forces in these transformations.

Finally, from a global perspective, the described state transformations are contributing to rising inequality between states. States like Norway, Canada or Japan have been consistently expanding state equity ownership over the last decades, while other (often austerity-plagued) governments increasingly withdrew from such investment, for example Greece, Ireland, Portugal and the UK (Kim 2021). The consequences of these diverging investment patterns are clear. Whereas Norway managed to become a heavyweight on global financial markets – despite being a small country and economy – others like Greece slipped into a financially subordinate position in the global economy. Such developments further exacerbate existing global inequalities. Many states that became successful owners do not only enjoy good credit ratings on financial markets, but can even to a large degree *directly* finance themselves as participants in these markets. We saw the examples of states as owners that were able to fill their budget gaps stemming from the Covid-19 stabilization expenses in Chapter 6. For other states that do not own such rainy-day funds, it is often even more difficult to refinance their sovereign debt via financial markets because of lower credit ratings and higher debt service costs. Although there are other ways of financing sovereign debt (such as common debt issuance mechanisms in the eurozone), this discrepancy between competing states and others that do not possess sovereign investment vehicles is certainly widening, especially for the Global South. To counter such developments, states like Angola, Gabon and Nigeria have created different sovereign investment vehicles, with mixed results so far (Markowitz 2020). As a bottom line, competing state transformations feed directly into increasing global inequalities. These effects are less pronounced in the existing literature on state transformations and hence represent a third major contribution to this body of knowledge.

All three aspects point out that the competing state transformation is an idiosyncratic one, since it does not seem to be in the first instance directly governance-related. By this I mean the fact that most state transformations are understood as transformations of authority and/or sovereignty (see Leibfried *et al.* 2015). In our case, the competing state cannot be easily qualified as such a transformation in the first place. States do not extend or qualify their sovereignty, nor do they significantly amend authority rights. By becoming large-scale owners and investors, they rather insert themselves into existing global market structures and exploit those through market mechanisms. States as owners do not "govern" markets but participate in them. These state transformations, however, have consequences related to issues of sovereignty and authority. The harsh reactions by some European governments and the US administration towards increased Chinese (state-led) overseas investment is a case in point (Babic & Dixon 2022). The reach of Chinese state capital into other jurisdictions has until recently not been treated as an extension of authority into these other states, but as yet another source of investment (see, e.g., Liu & Dixon 2021). Hence, global political and market actors are themselves still struggling to precisely understand the nature of state capital as oscillating between the logics of markets and states. For the discussions on state transformations, this means that we should pay attention to how states wield both political and market power, and how their interaction produces consequences that go beyond governance-related state transformations.

Existing critical political economy work on such transformations is a good place to start. Already early on, scholars like Weiss (2003, 2012) have pointed out that neoliberal globalization is not necessarily leading to a demise of state power, but rather to its transformation. Others like Block (2008) have even argued that "hidden" state forms such as a US developmental state were built during the heyday of neoliberal globalization. More recently, Baltz (2021) has proposed a differentiated view on the development of state capitalist capacities in the USA under Trump. Furthermore, Hameiri and Jones (2016, 2021) showed impressively how China's many state apparatuses and investment vehicles need to be disentangled if we want to understand the trajectory of Chinese foreign (economic) policy in the tension field between domestic development and hegemonic aspirations. Studies such as these are instructive for how future research on (competing) state transformations could be conducted in the following years. They pay attention to the tensions, ruptures, successes and failures of specific state apparatuses in dealing with domestic and global pressures and interest groups. They show that a classical view of states as unitary actors and markets as separate spheres of social activity does not get us far in understanding what state transformation in the twenty-first century really entails. Further research on the competing state and its upcoming transformations in an age of increased geoeconomic competition will profit from such perspectives. To conclude this book, I turn to the research prospects arising from the reported findings and the implications for policy-makers.

Beyond the competing state: a research agenda

This study aimed to outline the rise of transnational state capital and the competing state in a world in flux. I built the analysis on insights from the largest quantitative dataset on cross-border state investment, and described some of the global trends that emerged over the last two decades. Chapters 4 and 5 each provided a historical and qualitative analysis that complements this quantitative perspective. Chapter 6 looked at some of the most pressing issues of today's and tomorrow's international politics and assessed the role of state capital in these contentions. A future research agenda that builds on the findings of this book can develop these three topics, as I lay out in the following.

First, the role of state capital and state-led investment in the Covid-19 crisis needs to be thoroughly evaluated once the pandemic ends and pandemic-related fiscal measures have been phased out. At the time of writing (autumn 2022), Covid-related deaths are still a major concern across the globe, in addition to the human disaster and economic harm previous infection waves have caused. The state-led assistance and support for businesses and people that have been hit socio-economically by the crisis has already reached unprecedented levels. We can hence already say that state-led investment is and will play a major role in combatting the crisis and its fallout. It is crucial to not only claim a "comeback of the state" caused by Covid-19, but to precisely delineate where, how and to what degree states reinserted themselves as economic agents during and after the crisis. The analysis from Chapter 6 regarding the role of state capital in the crisis already presents a first step in this direction. Building on the distinction between different state investment strategies, future research could engage in better understanding the domestic effect of the success or failure of such strategies during Covid-19. The partial closure of the transnational agency space because of Covid-induced investment screening mechanisms for controlling strategies could, for example, lead to a stronger domestic reorientation of these strategies. Future research could observe whether such a reorientation of (state) capital flows is happening or not and what its possible effects are (going beyond the continuation of competing state politics). Furthermore, financial strategies could also come under increased strain in a world where funds for the rebuilding of domestic economies will be even more necessary after a prolonged pandemic. The function of sovereign funds as useful cash reserves could run out of steam if a contracting world economy brings in less profits and demands more domestic investment. Finally, a key question with regard to a post-pandemic world will be whether the new role many states as investors and saviours took on in the crisis will be permanent or not. Many observers evaluate the swift and decisive fiscal firepower of governments around the world as a potential rehearsal for the much more profound climate crisis that will require even higher levels of (green) state-led investment (Stern *et al.* 2021). Future research should pay attention to how this link is or is not established and whether a "permanent emergency state" can deliver on much-needed climate investment.

Second, the coming decade of geoeconomic competition can and should be scrutinized more thoroughly in future scholarship. In this study, I aimed to embed the role that state capital can and does play in the so-called new Cold War between China, the USA and their allies. I also argued that we should develop tools and perspectives that allow us to study the concrete shapes and forms of these new global rivalries and not just fall back to geopolitical metaphors. The approach I developed – studying the concentration of state-led investment – is a macro perspective that allows us to map where state capital is flowing and in which sectors and regions it concentrates. Such a mapping should be the first step in a broader endeavour to understand the dynamics on the ground. How exactly geoeconomic competition and change develop also depends crucially on local and regional alliances, overlapping or opposed actor interests and the strategic room for manoeuver different actors have in particular situations, be it the South China Sea, Arctic shipping routes or sub-Saharan African regions where rare metals are found. In Chapter 6, I described three cases of current and potential geoeconomic competition. This discussion was based on the previously employed mapping technique, which uncovered different sectoral and regional hotspots for competition. In a similar manner, future research can attempt to excavate cases where the concentration of state capital (or other forms of state-led involvement) creates patterns of cooperation between states as owners or investors. This will be especially interesting in cases where state actors collaborate on global (physical and digital) infrastructure projects that will shape the future of post-neoliberal globalization. The transportation and logistics of physical goods but also digital (financial) services and products will become more central in a hyperconnected, and at the same time increasingly competitive and hostile, international environment. Studies aiming to explore these patterns of geoeconomic competition, cooperation and conflict can draw on the arguments developed in this study and look beyond state actors.

Third, I highlighted and analysed the issue of climate change mitigation and decarbonization efforts from a state capital perspective. My analysis extended the environmental state literature to incorporate the long-neglected but vital aspect of states as global owners. I hold that the concentration of carbon ownership in the hands of state actors poses a strong potential for decarbonization efforts, since public demands can be more easily directed at state actors than at private companies producing, using and selling carbon products. I asked some open questions such as what exactly carbon capital is and what potential decarbonization strategies look like. From all three reviewed topics in this research agenda section, this is the most open and underexplored one. Future scholarship should engage in better carving out how and to what extent states are invested in carbon capital and how this carbon portfolio of states changes over time. In a similar vein, studies can engage in comparative work to carve out which state actors are especially prone to carbon investment and which strategies are more likely to be open for decarbonization efforts. Combining insights on carbon ownership profiles with other variables is also an important task. We need better insights into the state–society complexes governing carbon ownership and how possible decarbonization could or could not destabilize political and societal systems. In my analysis in Chapter 6, I touched upon this issue, which needs more exploration and regional expertise for all the different potential cases. The work conducted in this book provides a starting point to develop research designs and ideas that could facilitate our understanding and access to highly complex societal power relations that are often built on or are highly dependent on carbon capital. Finally, the connection between carbon state capital and other actors governing or owning carbon capital needs to be better scrutinized. My study focused on the state as owner, whereas the success of a green transition will also be crucially determined by the profitability and price of the non-state sector (see also Christophers 2022). The task of a state capital perspective can also be to excavate and study the links between state (capital) power and a still largely carbonized world economy. Future research will have to develop our understanding of how an expected demise of large parts of the (private) carbon industry might be accelerated, softened, replaced or otherwise influenced by the state as carbon (dis)investor.

This research agenda, based on the three themes discussed in Chapter 6, is already comprehensive, but of course it is not complete. Future research could engage in finding better ways of measuring state-led investment, especially over time; in clarifying the many relationships between state capital and non-state-owned capital; or in better understanding the socio-economic control of state capital through statist elites and how they differ in different contexts (or not). All this is certainly worthy of engagement, but it would easily exceed the scope of this chapter. I now turn to the insights policy-makers can potentially draw from the findings of this study.

Insights for policy-makers

Many of the discussions in this book are methodological, conceptual and empirical contributions to the IR and IPE literature on state-led investment and state transformations. State capital is a highly political and often politicized phenomenon. In recent years, not only commentators and observers but also policy-makers have been warning about the supposed state-based threats emerging from state-led investment (Espinoza 2020; Reuters 2020). State capital is, in these discussions, often viewed through the lens of a geopolitical dichotomy (Shih 2009): either state capital represents nothing but another type of investment that has to be treated as politically neutral, or it is another "tool" of statist and often authoritarian regimes that seek to project political power cross-border. This dichotomy is also reflected in debates between more liberal-leaning and mercantilist politicians and commentators that use stylized and abstract arguments of "free markets" versus "state interests" which underplay the messy and complex reality of state-led investment and the actors involved in it.

The first lesson from this book for policy-makers dealing with foreign state-led investment is to acknowledge this complexity and to move away from the geopolitical dichotomy described above. The case studies of Chapters 4 and 5 demonstrated that only in specific cases (see Russia and Gazprom) can we find truly geopolitical motives for cross-border state investment. The vast majority of cases of foreign state-led investment takes place for a variety of reasons which are to be located on a continuum from more to less strategic. Being strategic is not "political" per se, as it applies similarly to private and to state actors moving capital across borders. The exploration and discussion of various state investment strategies and how they can be (partially) explained by domestic circumstances illustrates this. Whereas state-led investment comes in a limited number of forms, it comes with a variety of reasons and motivations on the side of the investing state. Policy-making should take this into account when assessing state-led investment in specific cases.

The second lesson concerns the difference between states as owners, state investment vehicles and state investment strategies. As this study has shown, different analytical choices for mapping data and approaching states as owners have different advantages and drawbacks. As an example, I argued for an aggregation of investment ties at the national level for understanding which strategies states as owners tend to use on average (see Chapter 3). This is an *analytical* choice that allows us to see patterns on a global scale, but it is less useful for deducing generalized policy-related conclusions. Simply because states tend on average to use a certain strategy, it does not mean that every state investment and every state-owned vehicle will always stick to this strategy. This is important to understand in order not to mix up the causes and consequences of state-led investment. Policy-makers that are concerned with questions of long-term and large-scale developments in the global political economy can think of the strategic profiles of states as owners as a heuristic guiding their analyses. However, those that are concerned with specific investment deals on a daily basis should be aware that specific deals can and often do deviate from general patterns.

A third lesson following from the first two relates to the recent proliferation of investment screening mechanisms and the tendency to strengthen existing mechanisms, for example by lowering the investment thresholds for reviews (Bauerle Danzman & Meunier 2021). Policy-makers that are involved in setting up and fine-tuning these instruments need to make general decisions for transaction reviews that are taking place on a case-by-case basis. Screening mechanisms do not allow or forbid specific types of inwards investment, but they are designed to trigger a review process once specific thresholds or specific sectors are being targeted for investment by foreign actors. State-led and state-based actors play a delicate role in these reviews, since many screening mechanisms explicitly mention this type of actor as a potential security threat (broadly speaking) (see Babic & Dixon 2022). The trade-offs for policy-makers are clear. Already the triggering of a review process can mean both a delay for incoming investment as well as incurring problems for host and investment states: host states can appear as "economically nationalist", and investing states (or state entities) as potentially dangerous actors. The findings of this study can help policy-makers to integrate insights about *different* types of states as owners and state-based entities, and develop mechanisms that take these differences into account. This can help to avoid generalizations. As an example, instead of a generalization of "state-based threats" (UK Government 2017: 21) and the automatic triggering of review mechanisms, policy-making could triangulate insights about the overall strategy of specific states as owners, the specific investment threshold, the nature of the investment vehicle and the domestic situation of the host state. Some of this is already being implemented in screening mechanisms, for example the domestic situation of a host state by expanding or shrinking the scope of the sectors that fall under a mechanism. However, developments like the extraordinary employment of a national development bank by the German government to circumvent its own (apparently deficient) foreign trade laws in order to block a Chinese state-led investment in a German power grid network illustrate how screening loopholes can cause international political reverberations (Babic & Dixon 2022). The findings of this study propose a set of insights that could potentially guide a refinement of such mechanisms.

A fourth and final lesson is that the governance of state-led investment is almost absent on an international level. Except for loose, non-binding declarations of intent like the Santiago Principles for SWFs (IWG 2008), or particularized governance of SOEs as part of broader international investment agreements (Mendenhall 2016), there is no international framework governing state-led investment. The focus of this study was therefore on the non-governance aspects of state capital, and how it interferes with other politics on a global scale. Different from the general images of "state capitalism" and state-led investment as a supposed threat from the "East" and from authoritarian regimes (see Alami & Dixon 2020b), we can see that state-led investment is a much more variegated issue. Large states as owners like France, Norway and Canada show that state capital is a global phenomenon. Efforts to better regulate and govern state-led investment on a global scale could hence profit from the insight that such regulation should not only target the so-called usual suspects, such as China or the BRICS in general. Different from "punishing" these states as owners, global rules for the cross-border engagement of states as owners could in fact increase our knowledge and transparency about state capital globally. For such an approach to work it would be important to not fall back into creating specific rules for specific vehicles, as the definition of what, for example, an SWF is remains contested. The focus of this book provides policy-makers with an analytical scope that takes *states as owners* seriously, and could also inform future global efforts towards the more transparent regulation and governance of this phenomenon.

References

Note on data sources

Unless noted differently, all chapters draw on a dataset on cross-border state owner-ship that was created in 2018. It consists of cleaned and manipulated raw data from Bureau van Dijk's ORBIS database from December 2017. The data on the state as carbon owner in Chapter 6 consist of a second dataset which was created in 2021. This also draws on ORBIS data from August 2021. The codes used for cleaning, manipulating and analysing the data, as well as additional files and information on both datasets, can be found at: https://osf.io/wavtz/?view_only=b2bfa5fb28ed4 5b18f1fcb780bc71eb7.

Abdelal, R. (2015). "The multinational firm and geopolitics: Europe, Russian energy, and power". *Business and Politics* 17(3): 553–76.

Alami, I. *et al.* (2022). "Special issue introduction: what is the new state capitalism?" *Contemporary Politics* 28(3): 245–63.

Alami, I. & A. Dixon (2020a). "State capitalism(s) redux? Theories, tensions, contro-versies". *Competition & Change* 24(1): 70–94.

Alami, I. & A. Dixon (2020b). "The strange geographies of the 'new' state capitalism". *Political Geography* 82: 102237.

Alkadiri, R. & B. Ewers (2020). *Preparing National Oil Companies for a New Energy Landscape*. Boston Consulting Group.

Amar, J. *et al.* (2018). "Country factors and the investment decision-making process of sovereign wealth funds". *Economic Modelling*, S0264999317318254.

Andreff, W. (2015). "Maturing strategies of Russian multinational companies: compar-isons with Chinese multinationals". In D. Dyker (ed.), *The World Scientific Reference on Globalisation in Eurasia and the Pacific Rim*, 77–120. Singapore: World Scientific.

APE (2017). *Nos missions, notre doctrine*. Agence des Participations de l'État. https://www.economie.gouv.fr/agence-participations-etat/notre-mission-statement.

Arndt, H. (1994). "Full employment in historical perspective". *Australian Quarterly* 66(2): 1–12.

Arnold, T. (2020). "Sovereigns raid rainy day funds for $100 billion after COVID-19 storm". *Reuters*, 14 September.

Arvin, J. (2021a). "Norway wants to lead on climate change: but first it must face its legacy of oil and gas". *Vox*, 15 January. https://www.vox.com/22227063/norway-oil-gas-climate-change.

Arvin, J. (2021b). "Norway's trillion-dollar wealth fund sold the last of its investments in fossil fuel companies". *Vox*, 29 January. https://www.vox.com/22256192/norway-oil-gas-investments-fossil-fuel.

Asian Age, The (2017). "IB, Home Ministry red flag Essar–Rosneft deal". *The Asian Age*, 24 June. https://www.asianage.com/business/companies/240617/ib-home-minis try-red-flag-essar-rosneft-deal.html.

Atnashev, T. & T. Vashakmadze (2016). "Internationalization of Russian business: a double-headed strategy?" In R. Tulder *et al.* (eds), *Progress in International Business Research*, Vol. 11, 423–50. Bradford: Emerald.

Avi-Yonah, R. (2000). "Globalization, tax competition, and the fiscal crisis of the welfare state". *Harvard Law Review* 113(7): 1573–676.

Babic, M. (2021). "State capital in a geoeconomic world: mapping state-led foreign investment in the global political economy". *Review of International Political Economy*, online first. https://doi.org/10.1080/09692290.2021.1993301.

Babic, M. & A. Dixon (2022). "Is the China-effect real? Ideational change and the political contestation of Chinese state-led investment in Europe". *Chinese Journal of International Politics* 15(2): 111–39.

Babic, M., A. Dixon & I. Liu (eds) (2022). *The Political Economy of Geoeconomics: Europe in a Changing World*. London: Palgrave Macmillan.

Babic, M., J. Garcia-Bernardo & E. Heemskerk (2020). "The rise of transnational state capital: state-led foreign investment in the 21st century". *Review of International Political Economy* 27(3): 433–75.

Baltz, M. (2021). "What lies beneath the 'Tariff Man'? The Trump administration's response to China's 'state capitalism'". *Contemporary Politics* 28(3): 328–46.

Barclay Hedge (2019). *Hedge Fund Industry Assets under Management*. https://www.barclayhedge.com/solutions/assets-under-management/hedge-fund-assets-under-management/.

Baron, R. & D. Fischer (2015). "Divestment and stranded assets in the low-carbon transition". Background Paper for the 32nd Round Table on Sustainable Development. OECD. https://www.oecd.org/sd-roundtable/papersandpublications/Divestment% 20and%20Stranded%20Assets%20in%20the%20Low-carbon%20Economy%203 2nd%20OECD%20RTSD.pdf.

Barteczko, A., L. Kelly & J. Neely (2018). "Poland wants US sanctions to cover Nord Stream 2". *Reuters*, 29 January. https://www.reuters.com/article/us-europe-nordstr eam-usa-idUSKBN1FI134.

Bauerle Danzman, S. & S. Meunier (2021). "The big screen: mapping the diffusion of foreign investment screening mechanisms". *SSRN Electronic Journal*. https://doi.org/10.2139/ssrn.3913248.

Bergsten, C. (1996). "Competitive liberalization and global free trade: a vision for the early 21st century". Working Paper 96–15. https://www.piie.com/publications/working-papers/competitive-liberalization-and-global-free-trade-vision-early-21st.

Biebricher, T. (2018). *The Political Theory of Neoliberalism*. Stanford, CA: Stanford University Press.

Blake, P. & D. Wadhwa (2020). "2020 year in review: the impact of COVID-19 in 12 charts". World Bank blogs. https://blogs.worldbank.org/voices/2020-year-review-impact-covid-19-12-charts.

Block, F. (2008). "Swimming against the current: the rise of a hidden developmental state in the United States". *Politics & Society* 36(2): 169–206.

BMBF (2019). *A Franco-German Manifesto for a European Industrial Policy Fit for the 21st Century*. Berlin: Ministry of Economics and Energy. https://www.bmwk.de/Redaktion/DE/Downloads/F/franco-german-manifesto-for-a-european-industrial-policy.pdf%3F__blob%3DpublicationFile%26v%3D2.

BMWi (2019). *Investitionsprüfungen nach der Außenwirtschaftsverordnung (AWV)*. Federal German Ministry for Economic Affairs and Energy. https://www.bmwi.de/Redaktion/EN/Downloads/F/faq-zur-aussenwirtschaftsrechtlichen-investitionspruefung.pdf?__blob=publicationFile&v=2.

Bradshaw, M., T. Van de Graaf & R. Connolly (2019). "Preparing for the new oil order? Saudi Arabia and Russia". *Energy Strategy Reviews* 26: 100374. https://doi.org/10.1016/j.esr.2019.100374.

Braun, E., T. Larger & S. van Dorpe (2020). "EU big four press Vestager to clear path for champions". *Politico*, 6 February. https://www.politico.eu/article/eu-big-four-france-germany-italy-poland-press-executive-vice-president-margrethe-vestager-to-clear-path-for-champions/.

Braunstein, J. (2018). "Domestic sources of twenty-first-century geopolitics: domestic politics and sovereign wealth funds in GCC economies". *New Political Economy* 24(2): 197–217.

Bremmer, I. (2010). *The End of the Free Market: Who Wins the War between States and Corporations?* London: Penguin.

Buch-Hansen, H. & A. Wigger (2011). *The Politics of European Competition Regulation: A Critical Political Economy Perspective*. Abingdon: Routledge.

Cain, P. & A. Hopkins (1987). "Gentlemanly capitalism and British expansion overseas II: new imperialism, 1850–1945". *Economic History Review* 40(1): 1–26.

Cairncross, F. (2001). *The Death of Distance: How the Communications Revolution Is Changing Our Lives*. Cambridge, MA: Harvard Business School Press.

Caldecott, B. (2017). "Introduction to special issue: stranded assets and the environment". *Journal of Sustainable Finance & Investment* 7(1): 1–13.

Cantwell, J. & R. Mudambi (2000). "The location of MNE R&D activity: the role of investment incentives". *Management International Review* 40(1): 127–48.

Caon, V. (2020). "How Covid-19 is affecting FDI regulations". *Investment Monitor*. https://investmentmonitor.ai/manufacturing/how-covid-19-is-affecting-fdi-regulations.

Carney, R. (2018). *Authoritarian Capitalism: Sovereign Wealth Funds and State-Owned Enterprises in East Asia and beyond*. Cambridge: Cambridge University Press.

Cerny, P. (1997). "Paradoxes of the competition state: the dynamics of political globalization". *Government and Opposition* 32(2): 251–74.

Cerny, P. (2010). "The competition state today: from *raison d'état* to *raison du monde*". *Policy Studies* 31(1): 5–21.

CGCC (2020). *Chinese Enterprises in the United States*. Annual Business Survey Report. China General Chamber of Commerce. https://www.cgccusa.org/wp-content/uplo ads/2020/08/CGCC-2020-Annual-Business-Survey-Report.pdf.

Chen, C. (2016). "Solving the puzzle of corporate governance of state-owned enterprises: the path of the Temasek model in Singapore and lessons for China". *Northwestern Journal of International Law and* Business 36(2): 303–70.

Chen, C. (2013). "Corporate governance of state-owned enterprises: an empirical survey of the model of Temasek Holdings in Singapore". *SSRN Electronic Journal*. https://doi.org/10.2139/ssrn.2366699.

Chen, I. & A. Yang (2013). "A harmonized Southeast Asia? Explanatory typologies of ASEAN countries' strategies to the rise of China". *Pacific Review* 26(3): 265–88.

Choong, W. (2021). "Chinese–US Split is forcing Singapore to choose sides". *Foreign Policy*, 14 July. https://foreignpolicy.com/2021/07/14/singapore-china-us-southeast-asia-asean-geopolitics/.

Chowdhary, T. (2021). "Vattenfall CEO urges CFD support for German offshore wind". *Montel*, 13 January. https://www.montelnews.com/en/story/vattenfall-ceo-urges-cfd-support-for-german-offshore-wind/1186114.

Christensen, T. (2005). "The Norwegian state transformed?" *West European Politics* 28(4): 721–39.

Christophers, B. (2021). "The end of carbon capitalism (as we knew it)". *Critical Historical Studies* 8(2): 239–69.

Christophers, B. (2022). "Fossilised capital: price and profit in the energy transition". *New Political Economy* 27(1): 146–59.

Clark, G., A. Dixon & A. Monk (2013). *Sovereign Wealth Funds: Legitimacy, Governance, and Global Power*. Princeton, NJ: Princeton University Press.

Clark, G. & A. Monk (2010a). "Government of Singapore Investment Corporation (GIC): insurer of last resort and bulwark of nation-state legitimacy". *Pacific Review* 23(4): 429–51.

Clark, G. & A. Monk (2010b). "The legitimacy and governance of Norway's Sovereign Wealth Fund: the ethics of global investment". *Environment and Planning A: Economy and Space* 42(7): 1723–38.

Clark, S. (2021). "Sovereign-wealth funds invest more at home as Covid-19 hits economies". *Wall Street Journal*, 16 July. https://www.wsj.com/articles/sovereign-wealth-funds-invest-more-at-home-as-covid-19-hits-economies-11626427802.

Clinton, W. (2000). "Remarks at Vietnam National University in Hanoi, Vietnam. November 17, 2000". In *Public Papers of the Presidents of the United States: Administration of William J. Clinton 2000–2001*, 2547–51. Washington, DC: Office of the Federal Register National Archives and Records Administration.

CNBC (2019). "One of the world's biggest investors warns of low returns amid US–China trade war". *CNBC*, 2 July. https://www.cnbc.com/2019/07/03/singapore-gic-warns-of-low-investment-returns-amid-us-china-trade-war.html.

CNBC (2020). "Norway wealth fund earned a record $180 billion in 2019". *CNBC*, 27 February. https://www.cnbc.com/2020/02/27/norway-wealth-fund-earned-a-record-180-billion-in-2019.html.

Coe, N. (2014). "Missing links: logistics, governance and upgrading in a shifting global economy". *Review of International Political Economy* 21(1): 224–56.

Coe, N., P. Dicken & M. Hess (2008). "Global production networks: realizing the potential". *Journal of Economic Geography* 8(3): 271–95.

Cohen, E. (2007). "Industrial policies in France: the old and the new". *Journal of Industry, Competition and Trade* 7(3/4): 213–27.

Corden, W. (1984). "Booming sector and Dutch disease economics: survey and consolidation". *Oxford Economic Papers, New Series* 36(3): 359–80.

Coutant, H. (2014). *The State as a Holding Company? The Rise of the Agence des Participations de l'Etat in the French Industrial Policy.* Chicago: Society for the Advancement of Socio-Economics. https://hal.archives-ouvertes.fr/hal-02178873/document.

Crafts, N. (2006). "The world economy in the 1990s: a long-run perspective". In P. Rhode & G. Toniolo (eds), *The Global Economy in the 1990s*, 21–42. Cambridge: Cambridge University Press.

Crouch, C. (2011). *The Strange Non-death of Neo-liberalism.* Cambridge: Polity.

Crozier, M., S. Huntington & J. Watanuki (1975). *The Crisis of Democracy: Report on the Governability of Democracies to the Trilateral Commission.* New York: New York University Press.

Cuervo-Cazurra, A. (2018). "Thanks but no thanks: state-owned multinationals from emerging markets and host-country policies". *Journal of International Business Policy* 1(3/4): 128–56.

Daily Sabah (2019). "Russia's Sberbank closes deal to sell Turkey's Denizbank to Emirates NBD". *Daily Sabah*, 31 July. https://www.dailysabah.com/finance/2019/07/31/russias-sberbank-closes-deal-to-sell-turkeys-denizbank-to-emirates-nbd.

Dale, G. (2012). "Double movements and pendular forces: Polanyian perspectives on the neoliberal age". *Current Sociology* 60(1): 3–27.

Davies, W. (2017). *The Limits of Neoliberalism: Authority, Sovereignty and the Logic of Competition.* London: Sage.

Davies, W. & N. Gane (2021). "Post-neoliberalism? An introduction". *Theory, Culture & Society* 38(6): 3–28.

De Graaff, N. (2020). "China Inc. goes global: transnational and national networks of China's globalizing business elite". *Review of International Political Economy* 27(2): 208–33.

De Jong, B. & W. Zwartkruis (2020). "The EU regulation on screening of foreign direct investment: a game changer? *European Business Law Review* 31(3): 447–74.

DeLong, B. (2000). "What went right in the 1990s? Sources of American and prospects for world economic growth". In D. Gruen & S. Shrestha (eds), *The Australian Economy in the 1990s*, 8–23. Sydney: Economic Group, Reserve Bank of Australia.

Djankov, S. (2015). "Russia's economy under Putin: from crony capitalism to state capitalism". Policy Brief 15–18. Peterson Institute for International Economics.

Duit, A. (2016). "The four faces of the environmental state: environmental governance regimes in 28 countries". *Environmental Politics* 25(1): 69–91.

Duit, A., P. Feindt & J. Meadowcroft (2016). "Greening Leviathan: the rise of the environmental state?" *Environmental Politics* 25(1): 1–23.

EBRD (2020). *Transition Report 2020–21: The State Strikes Back*. European Bank for Reconstruction and Development. https://www.ebrd.com/news/publications/transition-report/transition-report-202021.html.

Eckersley, R. (2004). *The Green State: Rethinking Democracy and Sovereignty*. Cambridge, MA: MIT Press.

Eckersley, R. (2020). "Greening states and societies: from transitions to great transformations". *Environmental Politics* 30(1–2): 245–65.

Economist, The (2012). "The rise of state capitalism". *The Economist*, 21 January. https://www.economist.com/leaders/2012/01/21/the-rise-of-state-capitalism.

EDB (2021). *Singapore Economic Development Board*. Singapore: Singapore Government.

Eichengreen, B. & P. Vazquez (2000). "Institutions and economic growth in postwar Europe". In B. van Ark, S. Kuipers & G. Kuper (eds), *Productivity, Technology and Economic Growth*, 91–128. Berlin: Springer.

England, A. & A. Massoudi (2020). "'Never waste a crisis': inside Saudi Arabia's shopping spree". *Financial Times*, 24 May. https://www.ft.com/content/af2deefd-2234-4e54-a08a-8dbb205f5378.

Espinoza, J. (2020). "Vestager urges stakebuilding to block Chinese takeovers". *Financial Times*, 12 April. https://www.ft.com/content/e14f24c7-e47a-4c22-8cf3-f629da62b0a7.

EU Commission (2020). "Guidance to the member states concerning foreign direct investment and free movement of capital from third countries, and the protection of Europe's strategic assets, ahead of the application of Regulation (EU) 2019/452 (FDI Screening Regulation)". https://trade.ec.europa.eu/doclib/docs/2020/march/tradoc_158676.pdf.

Fan, Z. & S. Friedmann (2021). "Low-carbon production of iron and steel: technology options, economic assessment, and policy". *Joule* 5(4): 829–62.

Farrell, H. & A. Newman (2019). "Weaponized interdependence: how global economic networks shape state coercion". *International Security* 44(1): 42–79.

Feenstra, R., R. Inklaar & M. Timmer (2015). "The next generation of the Penn World Table". *American Economic Review* 105(10): 3150–82.

Fennell, P., S. Davis & A. Mohammed (2021). "Decarbonizing cement production". *Joule* 5(6): 1305–11.

Ferrera, M. & M. Rhodes (2000). "Building a sustainable welfare state". *West European Politics* 23(2): 257–82.

Fichtner, J. & E. Heemskerk (2020). "The new permanent universal owners: index funds, patient capital, and the distinction between feeble and forceful stewardship". *Economy and Society* 49(4): 493–515.

Fohlin, C. (2005). "The history of corporate ownership and control in Germany". In R. Morck (ed.), *A History of Corporate Governance around the World: Family Business Groups to Professional Managers*, 223–81. Chicago: University of Chicago Press.

Forster, T. *et al.* (2019). "How structural adjustment programs affect inequality: a disaggregated analysis of IMF conditionality, 1980–2014". *Social Science Research* 80: 83–113.

Foy, H. (2017). "Rosatom powers through nuclear industry woes". *Financial Times*, 27 June. https://www.ft.com/content/774358b4-5a4a-11e7-9bc8-8055f264aa8b.

Friedman, T. (2005). *The World Is Flat: A Brief History of the Twenty-First Century*. New York: Farrar, Straus & Giroux.

Garcia-Bernardo, J. *et al.* (2017). "Uncovering offshore financial centers: conduits and sinks in the global corporate ownership network". *Scientific Reports* 7(1): 6246. https://doi.org/10.1038/s41598-017-06322-9.

Genschel, P. & L. Seelkopf (2015). "The competition state: the modern state in a global economy". In S. Leibfried *et al.* (eds), *The Oxford Handbook of Transformations of the State*, 237–52. Oxford: Oxford University Press.

GeoPost (2018). "Parcels, even at the other end of the world". GeoPost, 10 July. https://www.groupelaposte.com/en/geopost--parcels-even-at-the-other-end-of-the-world.

Gerbaudo, P. (2021). *The Great Recoil: Politics after Populism and Pandemic.* London: Verso.

Gerschenkron, A. (1962). *Economic Backwardness in Historical Perspective: A Book of Essays*. Cambridge, MA: Harvard University Press.

Gertz, G. (2021). "Investment screening before, during, and after COVID-19". *Global Perspectives* 2(1): 24538. https://doi.org/10.1525/gp.2021.24538.

Gertz, G. & M. Evers (2020). "Geoeconomic competition: will state capitalism win?" *Washington Quarterly* 43(2): 117–36.

Geva, D. (2021). "Orbán's ordonationalism as post-neoliberal hegemony". *Theory, Culture & Society* 38(6): 71–93.

GIC (2008). *Report on the Management of the Government's Portfolio for the Year 2007/08*. Global Investment Corporation Singapore. https://www.gic.com.sg/wp-content/uploads/2021/03/GIC_Report_2008.pdf.

GIC (2021). *Report on the Management of the Government's Portfolio*. Global Investment Corporation Singapore. https://www.gic.com.sg/wp-content/uploads/2021/07/GIC_AR_PDF_210723.pdf.

Giddens, A. (2013). *The Third Way and Its Critics.* Cambridge: Polity.

Gill, S. (1998). "European governance and new constitutionalism: Economic and Monetary Union and alternatives to disciplinary neoliberalism in Europe". *New Political Economy* 3(1): 5–26.

Gills, B. (2008). "The swinging of the pendulum: the global crisis and beyond". *Globalizations* 5(4): 513–22.

Goldman, M. (2010). *Petrostate: Putin, Power, and the New Russia*. Oxford: Oxford University Press.

Goldstein, A. & P. Pananond (2008). "Singapore Inc. goes shopping abroad: profits and pitfalls". *Journal of Contemporary Asia* 38(3): 417–38.

Grätz, J. (2014). "Russia's multinationals: network state capitalism goes global". In A. Nölke (ed.), *Multinational Corporations from Emerging Markets: State Capitalism 3.0*, 90–108. London: Palgrave Macmillan.

Grugel, J., P. Riggirozzi & B. Thirkell-White (2008). "Beyond the Washington Consensus? Asia and Latin America in search of more autonomous development". *International Affairs* 84(3): 499–517.

Gürsan, C. & V. de Gooyert (2021). "The systemic impact of a transition fuel: does natural gas help or hinder the energy transition?" *Renewable and Sustainable Energy Reviews* 138: 110552. https://doi.org/10.1016/j.rser.2020.110552.

Haberly, D. & D. Wójcik (2017). "Earth incorporated: centralization and variegation in the global company network". *Economic Geography* 93(3): 241–66.

Hallaert, J. (2015). "Insights from the 19th century wave of bilateral trade agreements for the WTO era". *Trade, Law and Development* 7(2): 356–87.

Hameiri, S. & L. Jones (2016). "Rising powers and state transformation: the case of China". *European Journal of International Relations* 22(1): 72–98.

Hameiri, S. & L. Jones (2021). *Fractured China: How State Transformation Is Shaping China's Rise*. Cambridge: Cambridge University Press.

Hamilton-Hart, N. (2000). "The Singapore state revisited". *Pacific Review* 13(2): 195–216.

Hannas, W. & D. Tatlow (eds) (2020). *China's Quest for Foreign Technology: Beyond Espionage*. Abingdon: Routledge.

Hanson, P. (2007). "The turn to statism in Russian economic policy". *International Spectator* 42(1): 29–42.

Harper, J. (2020). "Is Saudi Aramco eyeing a step into Russia's backyard?" *DW*, 23 December. https://www.dw.com/en/is-saudi-aramco-eyeing-a-step-into-russias-backyard/a-56042138.

Harvey, D. (2011). *The Enigma of Capital: And the Crises of Capitalism*. Oxford and New York: Oxford University Press.

Hatzisavvidou, S. (2020). "Inventing the environmental state: neoliberal common sense and the limits to transformation". *Environmental Politics* 29(1): 96–114.

Hausknost, D. (2020). "The environmental state and the glass ceiling of transformation". *Environmental Politics* 29(1): 17–37.

He, X., L. Eden & M. Hitt (2016). "The renaissance of state-owned multinationals". *Thunderbird International Business Review* 58(2): 117–29.

Heimberger, P. (2021). "Corporate tax competition: a meta-analysis". *European Journal of Political Economy* 69: 102002. https://doi.org/10.1016/j.ejpoleco.2021.102002.

Helleiner, E. (1994). *States and the Reemergence of Global Finance: From Bretton Woods to the 1990s*. Ithaca, NY: Cornell University Press.

Helleiner, E. & T. Lundblad (2008). "States, markets, and sovereign wealth funds". *German Policy Studies* 4(3): 59–82.

Henderson, J. *et al.* (2002). "Global production networks and the analysis of economic development". *Review of International Political Economy* 9(3): 436–64.

Hendrikse, R. (2018). "Neo-illiberalism". *Geoforum* 95: 169–72.

Higgott, R. & N. Phillips (2000). "Challenging triumphalism and convergence: the limits of global liberalization in Asia and Latin America". *Review of International Studies* 26(3): 359–79.

Huber, E. *et al.* (eds) (2015). "Introduction: transformations of the state". In S. Leibfried *et al.* (eds), *The Oxford Handbook of Transformations of the State*, 1–32. Oxford: Oxford University Press.

Huff, W. (1995). "What is the Singapore model of economic development?" *Cambridge Journal of Economics* 19(6): 735–59.

Huijzer, M. (2021). "Ill-neoliberalism". *Krisis: Journal for Contemporary Philosophy* 41(1): 157–71.

Hults, D., M. Thurber & D. Victor (eds) (2012). *Oil and Governance: State-Owned Enterprises and the World Energy Supply*. Cambridge: Cambridge University Press.

IEA (2019). *Nuclear Power in a Clean Energy System*. International Energy Agency. https://iea.blob.core.windows.net/assets/ad5a93ce-3a7f-461d-a441–8a05b7601 887/Nuclear_Power_in_a_Clean_Energy_System.pdf.

IFSWF (2021). *IFSWF Annual Review*. https://www.ifswfreview.org/covid-response.html.

ILO (2021). *ILO Monitor: COVID-19 and the World of Work*, 7th edition. International Labour Organization. https://www.ilo.org/wcmsp5/groups/public/---dgreports/---dcomm/documents/briefingnote/wcms_767028.pdf.

IMF (2021). *Fiscal Monitor Database of Country Fiscal Measures in Response to the COVID-19 Pandemic*. IMF Fiscal Affairs Department. https://www.imf.org/en/Topics/imf-and-covid19/Fiscal-Policies-Database-in-Response-to-COVID-19.

Iwamoto, K. (2019). "Trade war hits Singapore's Temasek as returns plunge". *Nikkei Asia*, 9 July. https://asia.nikkei.com/Business/Business-trends/Trade-war-hits-Singapore-s-Temasek-as-returns-plunge.

IWG (2008). *Sovereign Wealth Funds: Generally Accepted Principles and Practices – Santiago Principles*. International Working Group on Sovereign Wealth Funds. https://www.ifswf.org/sites/default/files/santiagoprinciples_0_0.pdf.

Jessop, B. (2007). *State Power: A Strategic-Relational Approach*. Cambridge: Polity.

Johan, S., A. Knill & N. Mauck (2013). "Determinants of sovereign wealth fund investment in private equity vs public equity". *Journal of International Business Studies* 44(2): 155–72.

Jones, L. & S. Hameiri (2021). "COVID-19 and the failure of the neoliberal regulatory state". *Review of International Political Economy* 29(4): 1027–52.

Jones, L. & Y. Zou (2017). "Rethinking the role of state-owned enterprises in China's rise". *New Political Economy* 22(6): 743–60.

Jungbluth, C. (2018). *Kauft China Systematisch Schlüsseltechnologien Auf? Chinesische Firmenbeteiligungen in Deutschland im Kontext von "Made in China 2025"*. Gütersloh: Bertelsmann Stiftung. https://www.bertelsmann-stiftung.de/fileadmin/files/BSt/Publikationen/GrauePublikationen/MT_Made_in_China_2025.pdf.

Karimi, S. (2016). *Beyond the Welfare State: Postwar Social Settlement and Public Pension Policy in Canada and Australia*. Toronto: University of Toronto Press.

Kattel, R. *et al.* (2021). *The Green Giant: New Industrial Strategy for Norway*. Institute for Innovation and Public Purpose. https://www.ucl.ac.uk/bartlett/public-purpose/sites/public-purpose/files/thegreengiant_final_19_jan.pdf.

Katzenstein, P. (1985). *Small States in World Markets: Industrial Policy in Europe*. Ithaca, NY: Cornell University Press.

Kennedy, P. (1988). *The Rise and Fall of Great Powers*. London: Unwin Hyman.

Kessler, G. (2017). "The repeated, incorrect claim that Russia obtained '20 percent of our uranium'". *Washington Post*, 31 October. https://www.washingtonpost.com/news/fact-checker/wp/2017/10/31/the-repeated-incorrect-claim-that-russia-obtained-20-percent-of-our-uranium/.

Kim, K. (2021). "Locating new 'state capitalism' in advanced economies: an international comparison of government ownership in economic entities". *Contemporary Politics* 28(3): 285–305.

King, S. (2017). "The pendulum swings between globalisation and nation state". *Financial Times*, 19 April. https://www.ft.com/content/c497caf2-205a-11e7-b7d3-163f5a7f229c.

Klein, N. (2007). *The Shock Doctrine: The Rise of Disaster Capitalism*. London: Penguin.

Knolle, K. & P. Polityuk (2021). "Merkel defends U.S. Nord Stream 2 deal as Ukraine cries foul". *Reuters*, 22 July. https://www.reuters.com/business/energy/merkel-defends-us-nord-stream-2-deal-ukraine-cries-foul-2021-07-22/.

Kolodyazhnyy, A., O. Auyezov & L. Heavens (2021). "Rosatom, DP World to join efforts on Arctic container shipments". *Reuters*, 23 July. https://www.reuters.com/business/energy/rosatom-dp-world-join-efforts-arctic-container-shipments-2021-07-23/.

Krugman, P. (1994). "Competitiveness: a dangerous obsession". *Foreign Affairs* 73(2): 28–44.

Kundnani, H. (2020). "Europe after the coronavirus: a 'return of the state?'". IAI Papers. https://www.iai.it/en/pubblicazioni/europe-after-coronavirus-return-state.

Kurlantzick, J. (2016). *State Capitalism: How the Return of Statism Is Transforming the World*. Oxford: Oxford University Press.

Kus, B. (2006). "Neoliberalism, institutional change and the welfare state: the case of Britain and France". *International Journal of Comparative Sociology* 47(6): 488–525.

La Porta, R., F. Lopez-De-Silanes & A. Shleifer (1999). "Corporate ownership around the world". *Journal of Finance* 54(2): 471–517.

Lavenex, S. (2007). "The competition state and highly skilled migration". *Society* 44(2): 32–41.

Lee, Y. (2019). "A US–China deal that lacks trust could be 'dangerous,' warns Singapore's trade minister". *CNBC*, 2 September. https://www.cnbc.com/2019/09/02/us-china-deal-lacking-trust-is-dangerous-singapores-chan-chun-sing.html.

Leibfried, S. *et al.* (eds) (2015). *The Oxford Handbook of Transformations of the State*. Oxford: Oxford University Press.

Lekoy-Beaulieu, P. (1913). "Public ownership in France". *North American Review* 197(688): 295–311.

Levi, P. & J. Cullen (2018). "Mapping global flows of chemicals: from fossil fuel feedstocks to chemical products". *Environmental Science & Technology* 52(4): 1725–34.

Li, R. & K. Cheong (2019). *China's State Enterprises: Changing Role in a Rapidly Transforming Economy*. London: Palgrave Macmillan.

Lie, E. (2016). "Context and contingency: explaining state ownership in Norway". *Enterprise & Society* 17(4): 904–30.

Linsi, L. (2020). "The discourse of competitiveness and the dis-embedding of the national economy". *Review of International Political Economy* 27(4): 855–79.

Linsi, L. (2021). "Speeding up 'slowbalization': the political economy of global production before and after COVID-19". *Global Perspectives* 2(1): 24433. https://doi.org/10.1525/gp.2021.24433.

Linsi, L. & D. Mügge (2019). "Globalization and the growing defects of international economic statistics". *Review of International Political Economy* 26(3): 361–83.

Liu, I. & A. Dixon (2021). "Legitimating state capital: the global financial professions and the transnationalization of Chinese sovereign wealth". *Development and Change* 52(5): 1251–73.

Loong, L. (2019). "The impact of growing US–China tensions on Singapore". *Channel News Asia*, 19 August. https://www.channelnewsasia.com/commentary/us-china-singapore-trade-war-impact-businesses-growth-866571.

Lundberg, U. & K. Åmark (2001). "Social rights and social security: the Swedish welfare state, 1900–2000". *Scandinavian Journal of History* 26(3): 157–76.

Maddison, A. (1987). "Growth and slowdown in advanced capitalist economies: techniques of quantitative assessment". *Journal of Economic Literature* 25(2): 649–98.

Manley, D. & P. Heller (2021). *Risky Bet: National Oil Companies in the Energy Transition*. Natural Resource Governance Institute. https://resourcegovernance.org/sites/default/files/documents/risky-bet-national-oil-companies-in-the-energy-transition.pdf.

Mann, M. (2012). *The Sources of Social Power*, Vol. 3. Cambridge: Cambridge University Press.

Markowitz, C. (2020). "Sovereign wealth funds in Africa: taking stock and looking forward". Occasional Papers No. 304. South African Institute of International Affairs. https://media.africaportal.org/documents/Occasional-Paper-304-markowitz.pdf.

Mendenhall, J. (2016). "Assessing security risks posed by state-owned enterprises in the context of international investment agreements". *ICSID Review* 31(1): 36–44.

Menon, S. (2022). "Ukraine crisis: why India is buying more Russian oil". *BBC News*, 29 March. https://www.bbc.com/news/world-asia-india-60783874#:~:text=After%20the%20US%20and%20China,2%25%20of%20its%20total%20imports.

Meunier, S. (2014). "A Faustian bargain or just a good bargain? Chinese foreign direct investment and politics in Europe". *Asia Europe Journal* 12(1/2): 143–58.

Meunier, S. & K. Nicolaidis (2019). "The geopoliticization of European trade and investment policy". *Journal of Common Market Studies* 57(S1): 103–13.

Mihalyi, D., A. Adam & J. Hwang (2020). *Resource-Backed Loans: Pitfalls and Potential*. Natural Resource Governance Institute. https://resourcegovernance.org/sites/default/files/documents/resource-backed-loans-pitfalls-and-potential.pdf.

Mirowski, P. (2014). *Never Let a Serious Crisis Go to Waste: How Neoliberalism Survived the Financial Meltdown*. London: Verso.

Mommen, A. (2004). "Playing Russian roulette: Putin in search of good governance". In J. Demmers, A. Fernández Jilberto & B. Hogenboom (eds), *Good Governance in the Era of Global Neoliberalism: Conflict and Depolitisation in Latin America, Eastern Europe, Asia, and Africa*, 117–39. London: Routledge.

Naqvi, N. (2021). "Renationalizing finance for development: policy space and public economic control in Bolivia". *Review of International Political Economy* 28(3): 447–78.

Nelson, R. (ed.) (1993). *National Innovation Systems: A Comparative Analysis.* Oxford: Oxford University Press.

Nephew, R. (2022). "The wisdom of nuclear carve-outs from the Russian sanctions regime". *War on the Rocks,* 17 March. https://warontherocks.com/2022/03/the-wisdom-of-nuclear-carve-outs-from-the-russian-sanctions-regime/.

Neumann, A. *et al.* (2018). "Erdgasversorgung: Weitere Ostsee-Pipeline ist überflüssig". *DIW Wochenbericht* 27: 590–7.

Newnham, R. (2011). "Oil, carrots, and sticks: Russia's energy resources as a foreign policy tool". *Journal of Eurasian Studies* 2(2): 134–43.

Nölke, A. (2014). *Multinational Corporations from Emerging Markets: State Capitalism 3.0.* London: Palgrave Macmillan.

Nölke, A. *et al.* (2015). "Domestic structures, foreign economic policies and global economic order: implications from the rise of large emerging economies". *European Journal of International Relations* 21(3): 538–67.

Nölke, A. *et al.* (2019). *State-Permeated Capitalism in Large Emerging Economies.* Abingdon: Routledge.

Oatley, T. (2019). "Toward a political economy of complex interdependence". *European Journal of International Relations* 25(4): 957–78.

OECD (2020). "The impact of coronavirus (COVID-19) and the global oil price shock on the fiscal position of oil-exporting developing countries". OECD Policy Responses to Coronavirus (COVID-19). https://doi.org/10.1787/8bafbd95-en.

OECD (2021). "Statement on a two-pillar solution to address the tax challenges arising from the digitalisation of the economy". OECD/G20 Base Erosion and Profit Shifting Project, 8 October. https://www.oecd.org/tax/beps/statement-on-a-two-pillar-solution-to-address-the-tax-challenges-arising-from-the-digitalisation-of-the-economy-october-2021.pdf.

Olugbade, O. *et al.* (2021). "State-owned enterprises in Middle East, North Africa, and Central Asia: size, costs, and challenges". IMF. https://www.elibrary.imf.org/view/journals/087/2021/019/article-A001-en.xml.

Owen, G. (2012). "Industrial policy in Europe since the Second World War". ECIPE Occasional Paper, 1.

Parsons, T. (1999). *The British Imperial Century, 1815–1914: A World History Perspective.* Lanham, MD: Rowman & Littlefield.

Patton, D. (2018). "China-owned Syngenta plots growth in challenging home market". *Reuters,* 24 July. https://www.reuters.com/article/us-china-syngenta-idUSKBN1KE1B3.

Peck, J. (2001). "Neoliberalizing states: thin policies/hard outcomes". *Progress in Human Geography* 25(3): 445–55.

Peck, J. & A. Tickell (2002). "Neoliberalizing space". *Antipode* 34(3): 380–404.

Pek, S. (2017). "Economic Development Board". *Singapore Infopedia.* https://eresources.nlb.gov.sg/infopedia/articles/SIP_2018-2001-08_135544.html?s=Ministry%20of%20Trade%20and%20Industry.

Peng Er, L. (2021). "Singapore–China relations in geopolitics, economics, domestic politics and public opinion: an awkward 'special relationship'?" *Journal of Contemporary East Asia Studies* 10(2): 203–17.

Peters, J. (2008). "Labour market deregulation and the decline of labour power in North America and Western Europe". *Policy and Society* 27(1): 83–98.

Petry, J., J. Fichtner & E. Heemskerk (2021). "Steering capital: the growing private authority of index providers in the age of passive asset management". *Review of International Political Economy* 28(1): 152–76.

Phillips, A. & J. Sharman (2020). "Company-states and the creation of the global international system". *European Journal of International Relations* 26(4): 1249–72.

Pinchuk, D., J. Stubbs & H. Lawson (2016). "Rosneft-Essar deal not subject to sanctions: Russia's VTB head". *Reuters*, 15 October. https://www.reuters.com/article/us-essar-oil-m-a-rosneft-oil-sanctions-idUKKBN12F0JN.

Polanyi, K. (2001). *The Great Transformation: The Political and Economic Origins of Our Time*. Boston, MA: Beacon Press.

Porter, M. (1990). "The competitive advantage of nations". *Harvard Business Review* (March–April): 73–91.

Poulantzas, N. (1969). "The problem of the capitalist state". *New Left Review* 58(1): 67–78.

Quinn, J. (2008). "Citigroup and Merrill Lynch consult regulator on sovereign wealth funds". *The Telegraph*, 11 January. https://www.telegraph.co.uk/finance/newsbysector/banksandfinance/2782410/Citigroup-and-Merrill-Lynch-consult-regulator-on-sovereign-wealth-funds.html.

Railway Gazette (2012). "RZD to acquire 75% of Gefco". *Railway Gazette*, 20 September. https://www.railwaygazette.com/freight/rzd-to-acquire-75-of-gefco/37325.article.

Ren, D. (2019). "Singapore investors snap up US$5 billion of China's commercial properties, brushing aside trade war concerns". *South China Morning Post*, 15 June. https://www.scmp.com/business/china-business/article/3014477/singapore-investors-snap-us5-billion-chinas-commercial.

Reurink, A. & J. Garcia-Bernardo (2020). "Competing for capitals: the great fragmentation of the firm and varieties of FDI attraction profiles in the European Union". *Review of International Political Economy* 28(5): 1274–307.

Reuters (2012). "Edison says EDF bid not aimed at delisting". *Reuters*, 25 May. https://www.reuters.com/article/edison-idUSL5E8GPAFC20120525.

Reuters (2020). "Rubio unveils bill to kick blacklisted Chinese firms out of U.S. markets". *Reuters*, 27 October. https://www.reuters.com/article/us-usa-china-markets-idUSKBN27C25B.

Reuters (2021). "China was largest recipient of FDI in 2020". *Reuters*, 25 January. https://www.reuters.com/article/us-china-economy-fdi-idUSKBN29T0TC.

Reuters (2022). "Auto logistics firm Gefco to buy out Russian shareholder". *Reuters*, 1 April. https://www.reuters.com/article/gefco-rzd-idCNL5N2VZ33V.

Roberts, A., H. Choer Moraes & V. Ferguson (2019). "Toward a geoeconomic order". *Journal of International Economic Law* 22(4): 655–76.

Robinson, W. (2004). *A Theory of Global Capitalism: Production, Class, and State in a Transnational World*. Baltimore, MD: Johns Hopkins University Press.

Rodan, G. (2004). "International capital, Singapore's state companies, and security". *Critical Asian Studies* 36(3): 479–99.

Rosatom (2018). "ROSATOM plans to expand nuclear construction abroad". Rosatom press release, 3 July. https://rosatom.ru/en/press-centre/news/rosatom-plans-to-expand-nuclear-construction-abroad-/.

Ruggie, J. (1982). "International regimes, transactions, and change: embedded liberalism in the postwar economic order". *International Organization* 36(2): 379–415.

Schindler, S., J. DiCarlo & D. Paudel (2021). "The new Cold War and the rise of the 21st century infrastructure state". *Transactions of the Institute of British Geographers*, tran.12480. https://doi.org/10.1111/tran.12480.

Schindler, S. & J. Kanai (2021). "Getting the territory right: infrastructure-led development and the re-emergence of spatial planning strategies". *Regional Studies* 55(1): 40–51.

Scholte, J. (2005). "The sources of neoliberal globalization". Paper from the series Overarching Concerns, Programme Paper Number 8, United Nations Research Institute for Social Development. https://www.files.ethz.ch/isn/102686/8.pdf.

Schwan, M., C. Trampusch & F. Fastenrath (2021). "Financialization of, not by the state: exploring changes in the management of public debt and assets across Europe". *Review of International Political Economy* 28(4): 820–42.

Schwartz, H. (2012). "Political capitalism and the rise of sovereign wealth funds". *Globalizations* 9(4): 517–30.

Schwartz, H. (2018). *States versus Markets: Understanding the Global Economy*. London: Red Globe Press.

Shagina, M. (2020). "Double shock: the impact of COVID-19 and the oil price collapse on Russia's energy sector". Foreign Policy Research Institute. https://www.fpri.org/article/2020/06/double-shock-the-impact-of-covid-19-and-the-oil-price-collapse-on-russias-energy-sector/.

Shambaugh, D. (2013). *China Goes Global: The Partial Power*. Oxford: Oxford University Press.

Sheppard, D. & A. Raval (2020). "Rosneft warns BP and Shell creating 'existential crisis' for oil supplies". *Financial Times*, 28 September. https://www.ft.com/content/1394d8a1-6e85-451b-a858-ac6218b79d06.

Shields, M. (2017). "ChemChina clinches landmark $43 billion takeover of Syngenta". *Reuters*, 5 May. https://www.reuters.com/article/us-syngenta-ag-m-a-chemchina-idUKKBN1810CU.

Shih, V. (2009). "Tools of survival: sovereign wealth funds in Singapore and China". *Geopolitics* 14(2): 328–44.

Shiryaevskaya, A. & E. Mazneva (2021). "How Europe has become so dependent on Putin for gas". *Bloomberg*, 10 November. https://www.bloomberg.com/news/articles/2021-11-10/how-europe-has-become-so-dependent-on-putin-for-gas-quicktake.

Shleifer, A. & D. Treisman (2005). "A normal country: Russia after communism". *Journal of Economic Perspectives* 19(1): 151–74.

Shonfield, A. (1969). *Modern Capitalism: The Changing Balance of Public and Private Power*. Oxford: Oxford University Press.

Siddiqui, K. (2010). "The political economy of development in Singapore". *Research in Applied Economics* 2(2): 1–31.

Skidelsky, R. (2009). *Keynes: The Return of the Master*. London: Allen Lane.

Slobodian, Q. (2018). *Globalists: The End of Empire and the Birth of Neoliberalism*. Cambridge, MA: Harvard University Press.

Sommerer, T. & S. Lim (2016). "The environmental state as a model for the world? An analysis of policy repertoires in 37 countries". *Environmental Politics* 25(1): 92–115.

State Council (2017). "Building a world manufacturing power: premier and Made in China 2025 strategy". The State Council of the People's Republic of China. http://english.www.gov.cn/premier/news/2017/01/29/content_281475554068056.htm.

Stern, N., I. Patel & B. Ward (2021). "Covid-19, climate change, and the environment: a sustainable, inclusive, and resilient global recovery". *British Medical Journal* 2405. https://doi.org/10.1136/bmj.n2405.

Stewart, F. (2010). "Power and progress: the swing of the pendulum". *Journal of Human Development and Capabilities* 11(3): 371–95.

Stompfe, P. (2020). "Foreign investment screening in Germany and France". In S. Hindelang & A. Moberg (eds), *YSEC Yearbook of Socio-Economic Constitutions*, 79–115. Berlin: Springer.

Straits Times, The (2019). "Temasek looks to expand US investments regardless of trade war". *The Straits Times*, 20 November. https://www.straitstimes.com/business/economy/temasek-looks-to-expand-us-investments-regardless-of-trade-war.

Strange, S. (1996). *The Retreat of the State: The Diffusion of Power in the World Economy*. Cambridge: Cambridge University Press.

Strauss-Kahn, M. (2020). "Can we compare the COVID-19 and 2008 crises?" Atlantic Council blog. https://www.atlanticcouncil.org/blogs/new-atlanticist/can-we-comp are-the-covid-19-and-2008-crises/.

SWFI (2019). Chart of the Day, Sovereign Wealth Fund Assets under Management. https://www.swfinstitute.org/news/76389/chart-of-the-day-sovereign-wealth-fund-assets-under-management.

SWFI (2021). "Sovereign wealth funds are putting more money directly into biotech". Sovereign Wealth Fund Institute. https://www.swfinstitute.org/news/87769/sovere ign-wealth-funds-are-putting-more-money-directly-into-biotech.

Temasek (2021). "Portfolio performance". Temasek. https://www.temasek.com.sg/en/our-financials/portfolio-performance.

Thurber, M. & B. Istad (2012). "Norway's evolving champion: Statoil and the politics of state enterprise". In D. Victor, D. Hults & M. Thurber (eds), *Oil and Governance: State-owned Enterprises and the World Energy Supply*, 599–654. Cambridge: Cambridge University Press.

Tooze, J. (2014). *The Deluge: The Great War and the Remaking of Global Order, 1916–1931*. London: Viking.

Tooze, J. (2021). *Shutdown: How COVID Shook the World's Economy*. London: Viking.

UK Government (2017). "National Security and Infrastructure Investment Review Green Paper". Department for Business, Energy & Industrial Strategy. https://ass ets.publishing.service.gov.uk/government/uploads/system/uploads/attachment_d ata/file/652505/2017_10_16_NSII_Green_Paper_final.pdf.

UNCTAD (2011). *World Investment Report 2011: Non-equity Modes of International Production and Development.* https://doi.org/10.18356/6c9c5276-en.

UNCTAD (2019). *National Security-Related Screening Mechanisms for Foreign Investment.* Investment Policy Monitor Special Issue. Geneva: UNCTAD.

UNSD (2019). *UNSD Methodology.* Standard Country or Area Codes for Statistical Use (M49). https://unstats.un.org/unsd/methodology/m49/.

US Treasury (2021). "U.S. Department of the Treasury's Office of Tax Policy Meetings". https://home.treasury.gov/news/press-releases/jy0189.

Van Apeldoorn, B. (2002). *Transnational Capitalism and the Struggle over European Integration.* London: Routledge.

Van Apeldoorn, B., N. de Graaff & H. Overbeek (2012). "The reconfiguration of the global state–capital Nexus". *Globalizations* 9(4): 471–86.

Van Apeldoorn, B. & L. Horn (2018). "Critical political economy". KFG Working Paper Series, 87.

Van Miert, K. (1998). "What does a level playing field mean in the global economy?" European Commission. https://ec.europa.eu/competition/speeches/text/sp1998_031_en.html.

Verma, N. (2022). "India's Nayara buys Urals after 1 yr; IOC books another 3 mln bbls". *Reuters*, 24 March. https://www.reuters.com/business/energy/indias-nayara-energy-buys-urals-after-1-yr-sources-2022-03-23/.

Vernon, R. (ed.) (1974). *Big Business and the State: Changing Relations in Western Europe.* Cambridge, MA: Harvard University Press.

Viallet-Thévenin, S. (2015). "From national champion to international champion". *Revue Française de Science Politique* 65(5): 761–83.

Vogelsang, I. (1988). "Deregulation and privatization in Germany". *Journal of Public Policy* 8(2): 195–212.

Wang, Y. (2015). "The rise of the 'shareholding state': financialization of economic management in China". *Socio-Economic Review* 13(3): 603–25.

Webb, S. (1980). "Tariffs, cartels, technology, and growth in the German steel industry, 1879 to 1914". *Journal of Economic History* 40(2): 309–30.

Weber, I. (2021). *How China Escaped Shock Therapy: The Market Reform Debate.* Abingdon: Routledge.

Weiss, L. (2003). "Introduction: bringing domestic institutions back in". In L. Weiss (ed.), *States in the Global Economy: Bringing Domestic Institutions Back In*, 1–33. Cambridge: Cambridge University Press.

Weiss, L. (2012). "The myth of the neoliberal state". In C. Kyung-Sup, B. Fine & L. Weiss (eds), *Developmental Politics in Transition*, 27–42. London: Palgrave Macmillan.

Weiss, M. & M. Holter (2020). "Norway's $1 trillion wealth fund expands U.S. stakes amid rout". *Bloomberg*, 1 May. https://www.bloombergquint.com/business/norway-s-1-trillion-wealth-fund-expands-u-s-stakes-amid-rout.

Wigglesworth, R. (2020). "The index providers are quietly building up enormous powers". *Financial Times*, 20 January. https://www.ft.com/content/e761bdb2-33b3-11ea-9703-eea0cae3f0de.

Williamson, J. (ed.) (1990). *Latin American Adjustment: How Much Has Happened?* Washington, DC: Peterson Institute for International Economics.

Winecoff, W. (2020). "'The persistent myth of lost hegemony', revisited: structural power as a complex network phenomenon". *European Journal of International Relations* 26(1): 209–52.

World Bank (2020). "COVID-19 to add as many as 150 million extreme poor by 2021". World Bank press release. https://www.worldbank.org/en/news/press-release/2020/10/07/covid-19-to-add-as-many-as-150-million-extreme-poor-by-2021.

Wu, J. *et al.* (2021). "Evaluating the cumulative impact of the US–China trade war along global value chains". *The World Economy* twec.13125. https://doi.org/10.1111/twec.13125.

Wübbeke, J. et al. (2016). *Made in China 2025: The Making of a High-Tech Superpower and Consequences for Industrial Countries.* Merics Papers on China, No. 2. https://merics.org/sites/default/files/2020–2004/Made%20in%20China%202025.pdf.

Yang, H., P. Yang & S. Zhan (2017). "Immigration, population, and foreign workforce in Singapore: an overview of trends, policies, and issues". *HSSE Online* 6(1): 10–25.

Yasuda, A. (1993). "The performance and roles of Japanese development banks". http://www.ayakoyasuda.com/papers/performance_and_roles_of_japanese_development_banks_ocr.pdf.

Yergin, D. (2020). *The New Map: Energy, Climate and the Clash of Nations.* London: Penguin.

Zagha, R. (2005). *Economic Growth in the 1990s: Learning from a Decade of Reform.* World Bank Report. http://documents.worldbank.org/curated/en/664481468315296721/pdf/32692.pdf.

Zasiadko, M. (2020). "Arriva loses franchise in northern England". RailTech.com. https://www.railtech.com/policy/2020/01/29/arriva-loses-franchise-in-northern-england/?gdpr=accept.

Zhdannikov, D., N. Verma & K. Golubkova (2016). "Oil wars: how Kremlin's $13 billion Indian deal almost fell apart". *Reuters*, 29 November. https://www.reuters.com/article/us-russia-india-saudi-oil-idUSKBN13B083.

Zürn, M. & N. Deitelhoff (2015). "Internationalization and the state: sovereignty as the external side of modern statehood". In S. Leibfried *et al.* (eds), *The Oxford Handbook of Transformations of the State*, 193–220. Oxford: Oxford University Press.

Index